Moulded Clay

Eleazer Benenhaley

Psalm 107:8-9

Thank you for your hard work-
God Bless both of you!

Moulded Clay
Eleazer Benenhaley

Published by
DR. ELEAZER BENENHALEY
Sweetwater Rd., 180
North Augusta, SC 29841

Copyright 1983, 2019
Dr. Eleazer Benenhaley

Parts of this book were formerly published by
DANIELS PUBLISHING CO., INC.
1209 – 29th Street
Orlando, Florida 32802

Commendations

I have known Benenhaley as a roommate, fellow-student, beloved pastor and dedicated family man. Together, he and Nina have been a source of inspiration as we have labored together. This book will testify to the foundational truth that, Faithful is He who calleth you, who will also do it.

Rev. J. Larry Holland, Pastor
Franklin Heights Baptist Church
Rocky Mount, VA 24151

It is a great privilege to recommend to you Dr. and Mrs. Eleazer Benenhaley. It has been my joy through the years to count them among my dearest friends. I have watched them many times seek and follow the will of God for their lives in spite of many adversities. They have been an inspiration to my own life and ministry. Dr. Benenhaley is a powerful preacher with unwavering conviction as he stands true always to God's Word. Nina with her beautiful spirit has always stood with him in the gap. Let me recommend to you Moulded Clay from the pen of the faithful servant of the Lord.

Cr. Charles Page, Pastor
First Baptist Church
Charoltte, NC 29831

"It has been my joy to know Eleazer and Nina Benenhaley since 1976. Their Pilgrimage with out Lord has been a challenging and inspiring one. God has matured them through trials and struggles to be reflectors, as well as vessels, of His marvelous grace. Their deep wisdom is that kind which comes only from constant abiding in Christ and living daily in His Word. I commend this couple's testimony to you with full confidence that you shall be blessed by reading it again and again."

Arnold J. Becker
Director of Missions
Santee Baptist Association

Contents

Preface v

Introduction vii

Chapter 1
The Early Days Moving In 1

Chapter 2
The Beginning of School 3

Chapter 3
An Impact upon My Life 7

Chapter 4
A Life-changing Experience 9

Chapter 5
New Opportunities in Sumter County 12

Chapter 6
From School to Work 14

Chapter 7
The Girl Who Changed My Life 17

Chapter 8
Our First Home Together 21

Chapter 9
A Classroom in a Bus 24

Chapter 10
Preparation in the Church 26

Chapter 11
Preparation for School 29

Chapter 12
A Place Prepared by God 34

Chapter 13
Hard at Work...37

Chapter 14
Opportunities for Service in the Mountains 40

Chapter 15
Leaving the Mission..44

Chapter 16
Surprise at the Church 46

Chapter 17
Supply Preaching 48

Chapter 18
Sad News from Home..50

Chapter 19
My First Full-time Church....................................53

Chapter 20
Graduation Time...55

Chapter 21
Clear Creek's Impact upon My Life 57

Chapter 22
College-Bound..61

Chapter 23
A Loving Church 63

Chapter 24
A Tremendous Loss 66

Chapter 25
New Challenges during My College Days 68

Chapter 26
Staying at Concord...71

Chapter 27
Growing with the Students................................73

Chapter 28
Preparation for Seminary.................................79

Chapter 29
Entering Seminary 83

Chapter 30
Leaving Concord...87

Chapter 31
A New Church Field 91

Chapter 32
Leaving Siloam 99

Chapter 33
Ministering at the Long Branch Baptist Church............101

Chapter 34
A Time of Testing......................................105

Chapter 35
Seeking Ways to Broaden the Ministry of the Long Branch
Baptist Church...109

Chapter 36
Lessons Learned 113

Chapter 37
Leaving Long Branch....................................116

Chapter 38
Meeting the People at Sweetwater 121

Chapter 39
Moving to Sweetwater...................................123

Chapter 40
The First Months at Sweetwater 124

Part 2
Introduction 129

Chapter 41
Applied Ministry The Preacher 131

Chapter 42
Organizational Ministries Music Ministry 136

Chapter 43
Leaving the Parsonage A New Home 144

Chapter 44
Preparing to Leave Sweetwater 148

Chapter 45
To Silvercrest Meeting the Church Members 152

Chapter 46
Ministry at Red Hill Times of Heartache 156

Chapter 47
Conclusion 164

Dedication

To Nina, with love

A wife who exemplifies what the preacher has to say in Proverbs 3:10-20

Foreword

Dr. Delos Miles

"All theology, like all fiction, is at its heart autobiography," wrote Frederick Buechner. This is a volume of theology written as an autobiography. As such, it shows us through the life of one man and his family that "God is our refuge and strength, a very present help in trouble" (Psalms 46:1 RSV).

Read this book to see the faithfulness of God and the fidelity of his servants, Eleazer and Nina Benenhaley. Surely God has fulfilled His purpose for them and shown us through them how His steadfast love endures forever (see Psalms 138:8 RSV).

I have known Dr. Benenhaley for going on two decades, but I really gotten to know him through reading Moulded Clay. It is one of the finest autobiographies I have read. I wept and laughed my way through it, was inspired, informed and blessed by it.

Those who read this work are going to be surprised. I warn you to take off your shoes because you will be standing on holy ground. Prepare yourselves for a serendipitous experience. I found it to be a call to holiness, faithfulness and prayer.

Dr. Delos Miles
Professor of Evangelism
Southeastern Baptist Theological Seminary
Wake Forest, North Carolina

Dr. Terri Ann Ognibene

Moulded Clay 1 and 2 follows a man and his journey through life as he allows himself to be crafted by our living God. It is actually two books in one. Dr. Eleazer Benenhaley grew up in the rural south, during a time when he and his relatives were mistreated by society and denied an equal access to education. As a young man, he endured hard times and grew beyond the boundaries that society had placed on him, all the while giving praise to his heavenly Father for seeing him through life's difficulties and challenges.

Now that he has matured in life and in faith, he has endured many of life's other storms, and together, with his beautiful wife, Nina, and his family by his side, he prays that God will continue to shape him into the man that God wants him to be. Dr. Benenhaley is a humble servant whose gratitude for all of life's blessings is contagious. After reading this book, you are sure to have an attitude of gratitude!

This autobiography will entertain you, enlighten you and encourage you to look at the world through the lens of innocence and purity. It will also cause you to realize the importance of trusting God in all situations, knowing that He will see us through life's storms. Dr. Eleazer Benenhaley is proof that "in all things, God works for the good of those who love Him, who have been called according to His purpose" (Romans 8:28 NIV).

Dr. Terri Ann Ognibene
Spanish teacher
Pope High School
Marietta, GA
Co-author, *South Carolina's Turkish People,* published in 2018 by the University of South Carolina Press

Preface

How much value this book will have for others is not known. It is not being written from a stance of arrogance or self-importance. It is my desire that Christ might be glorified and that others might realize His purpose and plan for their lives.

We are living in a very confused world. Many people are living without any purpose, it seems. Secularism is dominating much of our society. The world, in many areas, is having more effect upon the church than the church is having upon the world. Many people have had it so good that they think they can get by without God. Some even have the nerve to say there is no God. Lines are being drawn in Christian circles, and it appears that many are more concerned about fighting each other than they are about fighting the devil. It appears that some theologians are more concerned about finding errors in the Bible than they are about teaching the precious truths of God's Word.

The idea for this book comes from what God has done in my life. As I look over my life, I see clay that was rough and wasting away. Within my own power, I never would have overcome the feeling of inferiority and a life relegated to second-class citizenship. What a difference when I met Jesus. He changed my life and gave me new purpose. Oh, I did not understand that purpose when I first accepted Christ, and I do not understand all that He has in store for my life after these many years of service. However, little by little, I began to see God's hand leading the affairs of my life.

If someone, who needs encouragement, reads this book and is blessed, I will be thankful. There are many who feel that everything has gone wrong, and I trust that they may see what God did in my life. He took events, which seemed like defeats, and He turned them into victories. He took impossibilities in my life and made them possibilities.

There is no way that I can thank all the people who have touched my life during these years. I am able to write this book because of school leaders, students, church members and friends. My mother always prayed and worked hard that I might be my best for the Lord. Her love and devotion are greatly appreciated. My wife and boys have given me the strength, by the help of God, to keep going. Nina is the kind of wife and mother who gives strength each day.

I would like to thank Mrs. Lois Morgan for reading the manuscript and for offering some very helpful suggestions and corrections. Mrs. Cindy Bolton labored hard in typing the manuscript. Both dear ladies are members of the Sweetwater Baptist Church, and I appreciate what they have done. Any mistakes are mine, and I take full responsibility for them.

Moulded Clay 1 and 2 are examples of God's miracles in the lives of my wife, Nina Benenhaley, and me. It is amazing how God can bring two people together and by His grace provide for them every step of the way.

Hopefully the travels, victories, trials and struggles of our family will be of help to those who might read these pages. When Nina and I moved to Kentucky, it was with fear and trembling because we did not know how we would be accepted. There is no way that we ever dreamed how kind, loving and protecting people have been in all the places where God has led us.

God was looking out for me when He gave me Nina. What a blessing she has been and is. She was both mother and father to our boys while I was in school. My boys, Clayton (deceased), Wilbur and Timothy have stood by and loved us. This does not mean that our boys always agreed when we moved from place to place. One deacon asked Nina, "Why are preacher's children so mean?" she replied, "Because they play with the deacon's children."

I want to thank Mrs. Beverly Reece and Dr. Terri Ann Ognibene for typing and editing this book. I take full credit for any mistakes.

God bless each reader who will let the Lord mould his or her life for His Glory!

Introduction

Paul uses the book of Romans to clarify the importance of God's leadership in our lives when he says, "Hath not the potter power over the clay, of the same lump to make one vessel unto honour, and another unto dishonour" (Romans 9:21 KJV). Any person who is surrendered to God, will cling to the words of Jeremiah 33:3 KJV, when he says, "Call unto me, and I will answer thee, and shew thee great and mighty things, which thou knowest not." These verses bring to mind my favorite verse, which says, "But my God shall supply all your need according to his riches in glory by Christ Jesus" (Philippians 4:19 KJV). As I look back over my life, it is so easy to see how God has worked so many things out, which seemed impossible in my life.

It is good that we do not know what the future holds for us. Neither our minds, nor our bodies, would be able to stand the pressures of knowing what each day holds for us. By looking at things from a spiritual vantage point, it is great to know Him who holds the future. There are those who want to claim that man is his own master and that his destiny is in his hands. If a person wants to believe that, it is his right. It is my right to believe that God has a plan for His children and that He will guide those who seek to follow Him. The person who does not accept the Bible as God's Word to his people will not agree with my view, but that still will not keep me from trusting His Word completely. There is much in the Bible that I do not understand, but I am still confident that His plan is being worked out in the lives of His children today. It is with joy and pride that I can say upon the authority of His blessed Word that I am His child. This cannot be attributed to any goodness of mine, but it can be attributed to the grace and mercy of God. I have no problem accepting the fact that our God is all-powerful and has a right to be in complete control of our lives.

Much has happened since the first part of *Moulded Clay* was written in 1982. These 36 years have been times of joy and sadness. Yet, through each year, God has been faithful.

In the second part of this book, hopefully, the years at Sweetwater, Silvercrest and Redhill will be helpful to those who read about the victories and struggles along the way. Thank God for His grace and mercy as He has protected and cared for my family and me all these years.

Part One

Chapter 1
The Early Days
Moving In

How far back can you remember? As one gets older, according to some, a person can remember those things that happened years ago better than recent events. Because of that fact, my attempt to write this story may be a sign that I am getting older. Just to set the record straight, there are many other physical signs that say that I am getting older.

My mother and father separated before I was born. Mother went to live with her parents near Wedgefield, South Carolina. When I was about three years old, my family moved to another farm near my birthplace. I can remember walking behind a mule-drawn wagon as my grandfather moved what little furniture we had to our new home. For twelve years, my grandfather was the only daddy I knew.

Those early years were lonesome, but good years for me. My mother never remarried. I learned how to survive. This was possible because we were a very close-knit family. Every person had his own job to do. Although I was small, I could carry in water and wood. Children of today do not have those types of responsibilities, and as a result, lose the opportunity of learning how to do things with their hands. Many children today would laugh at their parents if they were told to cut some wood or draw a bucket of water. Today's energy shortage might be ending that lack of knowledge.

We did not have the abundance of food or clothes that people so take for granted today, but we did appreciate what we had. Although she had a limited education, my mother worked at odd jobs to keep us going. Because we did live on a farm, we had our own hogs and chickens. Because of this, we had meat and eggs, which made the eating pretty good. There were times when I wished we did not have them because it fell my lot to feed them. I do not suppose you could really call me lazy, but on second thought, I probably would not have won first prize for being the smartest boy around, either.

Not many people would have been envious of my early social life. The days were long and often very boring. When some of my relatives came to visit, my day was brighter. Some of my cousins thought those visits were a boring time because I hid some of my toys. Well, after all, things were tough, and I could not let those roughnecks destroy my hard-to-come-by playthings. We laugh about it now, but I suppose my cousins did get rather angry when they saw me hiding my toys.

When I was alone at home, I became Superman, the Long Ranger and all the comic and radio heroes. My gun was a piece of tin. I would beat that tin with a stick and you would have thought Wedgefield had been attacked by a foreign power. My frustrations of being alone did not have time to build up because I let them out on that tin. It is a good thing that no mental health people were in the area at the time. Had they been, I probably still would be in the mental institution.

My boys like what some people call music today. You mothers and fathers know what I mean. You cannot make any sense out of it, but it is called music. On the other hand, had one of these present-day music directors found me when I was beating on that tin, I might be rich today.

My uncle, Woodrow Hood, who was in the Navy at the time, bought me a big tricycle and did I think something of that three-wheeler! It had brakes on the cross bar. As children came to visit, they were excited when I would let them take a ride. Then there were times when my selfish streak would take over, and I would not let anyone ride. Those types of playtime and visits from my relatives helped me keep my sanity during those early years of development.

Chapter 2
The Beginning of School

When time came for me to attend school, it was a day of excitement for me. It was also a time when I had to stay with my aunt if I planned to get to school on time. My farm home was too far from the bus stop for me to travel by myself. Mother could not walk the mile with me because she was working. My cousins met the bus with me that September morning in 1940. Little did I know, at the time, the surprises that were in store for me at the Dalzell School for Turks.

The Dalzell School had been provided for the people living in Sumter County whose ancestral background was Turkish. I was too young to understand the hatred and prejudice that had developed against the people of my ancestral background by some living in the area. It is so tragic that people let their feelings color their intelligence. This feeling of superiority by some deprived many Turkish children of a good education. Any educated person knew then, and knows now, that the Turkish people belong to the Caucasian or white race.

What a breathtaking sight when I arrived at the Dalzell School that beautiful morning. Standing majestically by the road was a white-framed building with a green top. This marvelous building had three rooms and even had a lunchroom. The Sumter County School District could be proud of providing such a marvelous school for second-rate citizens. There were three teachers for eleven grades. However, there was no running water and the students had to bring in coal and wood to fuel the stoves. The teachers did their best with the materials that were provided. I spent ten years of my life studying at Dalzell, and it had a profound effect on my ability to compete in a world where an all-around education is needed.

My first-grade teacher was a lovely lady, and I think she did her best for us. Most of the students could read their Dick and Jane books without looking at the pages. It was not surprising for a student to be caught looking out of the window when it was time for him to read, but he would not miss a word. One of the best times of school was when the Bible teacher would come. Thank God for those teachers who taught the Bible. Many children are being robbed today because some have said that it is against the law to read the Bible and have prayer in public schools. The Constitution does not forbid Bible reading or prayer in schools. The person who says it does, in my opinion, is going beyond what the writers of that great document intended.

Playtime at Dalzell was something. The students would have to determine the games. The school district did not provide any playgrounds or materials. When we played ball, we would use a rubber ball that someone had brought from home. If you wanted to see something exciting, you watched as the older boys played cowboys. They used stick guns cut from tree branches. A few fellows were fortunate enough to have a cap pistol. Prison base was a fun game for many. This game really proved how fast a person could run. The brave boys would participate in boxing. The rules were that no one should hit the other in the face. You see, the boxers were using their naked fists. The bout would not be started well before some smart fellow would let the other one have it right square on the jaw. This usually would discourage further boxing matches that day.

Graduation was an exciting time at Dalzell. Even though the eleventh-grade diploma that was granted would not be valid for college entrance, each person who received one was happy because he had worked very hard. It is so tragic that these students could not have received the same diplomas that were given at Hillcrest and Edmunds High Schools. In fact, they would have, had they been given their rights.

The small stage room would be packed. Usually, in addition to the graduation ceremonies, different classes would put on some type of play. The diplomas given by the district were second-class, but the job done by the students under difficult circumstances was first-class. One must wonder, if those students had been given the same opportunities as those at Hillcrest and Edmunds, what places of leadership would they hold today? Those who deprived these students of their rights because of prejudice will have to answer to God one day.

At Dalzell, I was an average student through the first eight grades. Due to the lack of space, some of us had to stay in the third grade for two years. To ease the pain to our ego, the teachers stated that a small third grade and large third grade were being established. They probably felt that this would be better than saying we had failed. To be honest, we had not failed. Our grades were plenty good enough for us to move to the fourth grade. This fact did not ease the pain of having to spend another year in the same grade. It was frustrating and degrading.

By the time I reached the ninth grade, I did not know a noun from a pronoun. This was not due to mental inability, but to the fact that we had not been taught the essentials of grammar. My ninth-grade teacher was very good, and she began to help us in these areas. The ninth through the eleventh grades used the same book. Alston, who was an eleventh grader, sat right behind me and when the teacher would ask me a question about nouns or pronouns, he would give me the wrong answer. The tragic thing is that I did not know any better. Consequently, when I completed the ninth grade, my grasp of the English language was very poor.

Many other important subjects were very inadequately taught. My knowledge of science was very limited because our study of the subject was limited. There were no research books and the only microscope at the Dalzell School was a picture in the science book. I am not sure that the book even had a picture of one. Can you imagine a student going through eleven years of schoolwork and never having the opportunity to see living things move under a microscope? God only knows what some students could have become, had they had a chance. As I look back over those years and realize how much I missed, it is hard not to be bitter. There is the old sinful nature, which says, "Blame others", but my Lord has taught me that you do not win by blaming others or holding grudges. If I were not a child of God, I could not help but blame others.

Back during the late forties and early fifties, I listened excitedly to the Sumter American Legion baseball games over the radio. I never saw a game, but I dreamed of what it would be like to have a uniform and step out on the diamond. Young boys of Turkish descent could not take part because they were not wanted, and no one had ever shown them the essential rules of baseball. Think of it now, eleven years of school and not one coach to show a boy how to hold a bat or how to throw a curve ball. You can only wonder how many major league prospects were never found.

For some Sumter County residents, the schooling at Dalzell is all they could afford. Many have made the best of a tragic time in their lives. Some will say that it was better than nothing, and this is true, but it still does not exonerate those who made such a school a part of the community. It is a blight on a community that never should have occurred.

There are still some today who will use the term, "Turk", with a slur or disdain but they should be pitied rather than condemned. Every person in Sumter County, who is of Turkish descent, has every right to be proud of who he is. What other family group in Sumter can trace their ancestry farther? Parks and schools are named after General Thomas Sumter, but what other group can claim closer association with the General than the people of Turkish descent? It might enlighten many people in the Sumter area if they would read what General Thomas Sumter's great-grandson, Thomas Sebastian Sumter, had to say about the Turkish people in his book, *Statesburg and Its People*. Anne King Gregorie gives an account of the Turkish people in her book, *History of Sumter County* (1954, 467). Much of her information comes from *Statesburg and Its People*. Robert Bass gives similar information in his book, *Gamecock* (1961, 78). The latest history to mention the Turkish people is Cassie Nicholes in her book, *Historical Sketches of Sumter County: Its Birth and Growth* (1975, 136). These books were limited in their treatment of the Turkish people because of lack of communication.

Chapter 3
An Impact upon My Life

Most children take for granted the blessing of being brought up in a home where both parents share their love. My grandfather was the only father I knew since my mother and real father had separated before I was born. My grandfather was a real father and pal to me. It was a joy for me to take breakfast to the cotton gin or to the field where he was plowing. He let me ride on the drag plow in the evenings when I would be returning from school. At night, I enjoyed the stories he would tell before bedtime. We walked for miles to fish at Thomas Lake or Beech Creek. It was just fun to be with him and talk about fishing and hunting. I was too small to own a gun, but he let me go squirrel hunting with him. Although I was just a boy, I learned things from him, which would be helpful later.

My grandfather had not lived a life about which he was proud to talk. He was a hard worker, but old Satan had led him astray in many areas. One night during revival services at Long Branch Baptist Church, he walked the aisle and gave his heart and life to the Lord Jesus Christ. What a change that took place in his life! He would talk to me about the love of Jesus until tears would run down his face and drop on the floor. During this time in his life, grandfather got sick. The doctor finally realized that it was cancer. Years before, grandfather had fallen and knocked most of his teeth loose. Whether that accident had anything to do with his getting cancer, we will never know. The Lord was so precious to grandfather during his time of sickness. A non-Christian would not be able to understand how Jesus could be precious during a time of intense pain. He might even question the goodness of God. Too many people blame God for the agony that many suffer. Grandfather had cancer when many of the painkillers of today were not available. I remember him saying when he was in terrible pain, "The Lord will not let me continue to suffer like this." It would not be long before he would drift off to sleep. That faith of his, during those trying times, has been a source of strength for me. He grew steadily worse and when he began to hemorrhage, mother knew that he would have to be taken to the hospital. Grandfather came through the room where grandmother and I were sitting and said, "If I never see you again, meet me in Heaven." My grandfather lived to come home again, but when he did die, no one had to convince me that he had gone to Heaven. Yes, he had lived a life that had been controlled by Satan, but thank God, he brought his sins to the Lord Jesus Christ and was abundantly pardoned. He had been forgiven of all the wrongs that he committed. "Therefore, being justified by faith, we have peace with God through our Lord Jesus Christ" (Romans 5:1 KJV). When grandfather died, I was twelve years old. His death left a very empty spot in my life, but God took care of me. God has so many ways of touching our lives. Some call it fate, but I say that God has a plan for His children.

Before grandfather died, he gave me a pig to raise. After his death, I sold the pig and bought myself a beautiful bicycle. My uncle rode it from Sumter for me. I kept that bicycle until I was 17 years old.

Chapter 4
A Life-changing Experience

The school year 1949-50 was my last one at Dalzell. During March of 1949, I accepted Jesus Christ as my Lord and Master. Some of my friends at school and church had urged me to join the church. Morally I was a good boy, but I did not know Jesus Christ as my personal Savior. If good works could have saved, I would have been all right, according to most people. Many fail to realize that we do not have any goodness of our own. If we are good, it is because the Lord has made us so. Oh yes, I went to church and could quote you scripture, but I was just as lost as could be. One day as I listened to a radio preacher, (that is right, I was not in church), I bowed my head and surrendered to my Lord. The Lord had plans for my life, and I did not realize it at the time. That afternoon I could hardly wait to get home and tell my mother the good news. That night I did not use the "Lord's Prayer" but opened my heart in prayer to my Lord. What a joy it was to talk with my Lord and realize that He heard me. For some reason I did not attend school the next day, but I walked the mile to the bus stop to tell a close friend about my new relationship with Jesus Christ. My life had taken a turn down a new road, and the Lord controlled that road.

Because my mother was concerned about the type of education that I was receiving at Dalzell, she made plans for me to attend school in Columbia, South Carolina. She had been seeking ways to get me enrolled at the Opportunity School in West Columbia. When mother contacted Dr. Wil Lou Gray, the director of the school,

Dr. Gray informed mother that I would be accepted. It was good to know that there were those who were not prejudiced against me because of my name or ancestral background. In fact, no area outside of Sumter County gave the Turkish people any problem about attending school.

When mother and I left for the Opportunity School, although it was only about fifty miles away, it appeared that we were going out of the state. To my knowledge, I had never been to Columbia before. During those days, farm children did very little traveling. Dr. Gray and her staff accepted us very graciously when we arrived. Mother stayed just long enough to get me introduced to my new family. Oh, how my heart sank when mother turned to leave me at the school. The only time I had been away from home before this was to stay with some relatives. It seemed as if my world had caved in. Sure, I should have been happy for a new chance for an education. Some sixteen-year-olds probably could have handled the situation beautifully, but I was not that mature. My disappointments were just beginning. My Lord, I think, was trying to teach me a lesson about patience. In order to find my grade level, I was given a battery of tests. This was new to me. Although I had been in school for ten years, I had never been exposed to such tests. Frustration really set in when I was placed in the sixth grade. If you want your ego deflated, let someone tell you that you are three grades behind. This was not the end of the world because the work could be made up. The truth of making the work up never got through to me. I never got over the disappointment of my grade level. I felt hurt and cheated.

The school officials were super. They tried to make me feel at home. A job was provided so I could pay my way through school. It was my responsibility to work in the kitchen. This required my being there before and after classes. You should have seen me operating that big dishwasher. I broke enough dishes to get fired. At the end of the week, I was given enough money to buy some refreshments. This was great, but I was told that I would not be able to go home every weekend. This just would not do. Being fifty miles from home during the week was bad enough, but to stay on the weekend was too much. Now you just do not hold down a sixteen-year-old boy who is in the sixth grade. Any person with that much smarts should be able to figure out a way to get home. It was not long before I had the perfect reason for going home. It was October, and the nights were chilly. You see, I did not bring any blankets and had been sleeping between the mattresses. When I informed Dr. Gray of this emergency, she was very understanding and let me go home. Let me tell you, when I left the school that Saturday morning, I would not have been any happier had I been to London. It was great to get home. After all, it had been five days since I saw my family. It seems so funny now, but it sure was not funny back then. I felt very important when I attended church on Sunday, but my dread of going back on Monday soon overcame that important feeling. I blew the opportunity the school had provided for me. After five weeks, I quit. This was to be a trademark of mine for some time.

    I cannot undo those mistakes I made, but I do hope that others might see where I failed and avoid making the same mistakes. At the time, I was thinking about my own feelings. As a result, I failed to realize the hurt and embarrassment I must have caused my mother. She had worked so hard to provide for me and now I had let her down. Many students would have gladly used the opportunities that I let slip away. Mother did not tell me how ignorant I was for dropping out of school. She was much more understanding with me than I would have been if it had been a child of mine.

Chapter 5
New Opportunities in Sumter County

When the young men of Turkish descent returned from World War II, they found that they could not attend school with their friends with whom they had served during the war. In the past, because of their lack of education, the Turkish people had almost a fatalistic attitude about life. They did not appreciate the way they were treated, but they did not know what to do. This attitude changed after the war, and the people demanded their rights to a better education.

The Turkish people took their case to court, and in 1951, they were admitted to the all-white high schools of Sumter County. The struggle through which these dedicated people labored made it possible for me to have another chance at a good education.

Since I lived near Wedgefield, I enrolled at Edmunds High School in Sumter. My first day at Edmunds was a time of nervousness and frustration. This in no way was the fault of the school administration. It was due to the fact that I was not ready for such a change. The Dalzell School had about sixty students and now I had been placed with about 900 students. I was afraid and felt very much alone. When I did get my books and was placed in the 10th grade class, it did not take me long to realize how unprepared I was. The administration tried to help in every way possible. I tried the classes for five weeks and let the defeatist attitude take control again. Every class and function of the school was open to me. The football coach wanted to know if I wanted to go out for football, and I said "no." At that time, I did not realize the opportunities that I was passing up. Some of my friends in the county high school were not treated nearly as kindly. In fact, they were not permitted to play ball or take part in certain class functions. During the five weeks that I attended Edmunds High School, not one student or teacher ever mentioned that I was Turkish or showed any signs that I was not welcome. When I finally decided that I was going to quit, my mother let me know, in no uncertain terms, that I was going to work. When I went to the office to turn in my books, my teacher talked me out of quitting. That is, she did while she was in the room. I told her that I planned later to attend some Bible school. I was not really lying to her, but I did not know of any Bible school at the time. That same evening when my teacher was not looking, I went by the office and signed out. It appeared that I was headed for a life of failure. My grades testified to that fact. I try not to reminisce on my past failures too much, but, at times, I do wonder how it could have been had I taken advantage of those early opportunities. What would it have been like had my early school days started in a good school? It would not be fair to blame all my failure on the happenings at Dalzell School and those who forced me to attend such a school. However, it is fair to say that it never should have happened. Thank God, we are living in a more enlightened day now. Young people have tremendous opportunities today, and many are not taking advantage of those opportunities.

Chapter 6
From School to Work

When mother stated that I was going to work, she was not kidding. She had a job waiting for me when I got home from school. My experience with work consisted of working on the farm and taking care of my uncle's chicken farm. Mother got me a job working in a grocery store. The responsibilities falling on my shoulders were to keep the store clean and the shelves filled with groceries. The boss was rather crabby, but what else could a quitter expect? Things went along very well until I was told to put some beer in the cooler. This shocked me because I did not know the owner sold beer. I was only 17 years old, but I knew that my Lord would not be pleased. I thanked the owner for the job and told him that I would not be back the next day. Some of my friends told me that there was nothing wrong with handling beer if I did not drink it. In my opinion, if it was wrong to drink it, it was wrong to handle it. How could I tell people that I was a Christian and handle something that destroys lives and families? My convictions are just as strong today about the use of, or handling, beer. A person who has been redeemed should stay away from anything that would hurt his testimony for the Lord.

    A large construction job had begun at Shaw Field, but I was not sure if I was old enough to get a job. My uncle, with whom I lived, had already gotten a job with the company. On a very cold January morning, I went to the construction site to see if I could be hired. While a group of us waited to see the foreman, we built a fire to keep warm. After waiting part of the morning, my uncle's foreman came and hired me. Let me tell you – he gave me a job. I carried enough nails and lumber to cause the foreman to see that I really wanted to work. My luck was very good that day. I walked into a two-by-four and broke my glasses. It took just about a week's work to get them fixed. The job lasted for several months. Although I was small, I could do my share of the work.

During the summer, we had to lift ready-prepared rafters onto the roof of the building. The July weather was terrible. Some of the men could not stand the heat and had to fall out. At the time, I thought I was really strong and smart because I could continue to work. Now I am not so sure. In fact, I wonder if those men were exhausted. Later I was given a job as a carpenter's helper. This gave me the opportunity to learn more about building.

Up until this time, my means of travel was walking, riding a bicycle or catching a ride with someone. In order to get to work, I rode with a cousin of mine. When I went to church, I would have to ride with someone or ride my bike. Mother and grandmother did not have any way to get to church. Since I had been working, I saved a little money to put on a car. Mother and grandmother chipped in also. A friend helped me find a 1940 Mercury. I was in class now. Not only could we go to church, but also, I might be able to get a girl to ride with me. That is, if she did not value her life too highly.

It is a good thing that God takes care of His own. He cares for us even when we are foolish. This does not mean that He will not allow us to hurt ourselves. Many times, I did some very foolish things with my car and I know that God had to protect me. I had a very heavy foot on the gas. As I look back now, I can see that the Lord was protecting me because he had a particular job for me. How I thank Him for the opportunity to serve. I feel so inadequate at times, but He gives me strength to keep on. My mother and grandmother were so thankful that they were able to attend church and, on occasions, visit some friends.

That 1940 Mercury taught me many lessons. It did not take me long to realize that it would not run off air. I also found out that you pay for abusing a car. I failed my license-driving test twice in Sumter. I was so green about town parking that I did not know what the police officer meant when he told me to parallel park. I just backed the car between the bars. Needless to say, I did not get my license. If it had not been for the station in Eastover, I do not know when I would have gotten a license.

Chapter 7
The Girl Who Changed My Life

It is very romantic when a young man marries his boyhood sweetheart. It was not this way with Nina and me. I had known Nina since we were children, but there was not the slightest idea of being sweethearts. We visited the home of each other and worked together in the fields. We attended school and church together but the farthest thing from our minds was marrying each other. Nina and her sister would meet the school bus with me. This meant that they had to walk about two miles to catch the bus. Because of this, Nina and her sister had to drop out of school because the distance was too great for girls to travel by themselves.

By the time I was 17 years old, my interest in Nina had changed. I suppose I was, at last, beginning to grow up. I spent more time at Nina's home. She may have thought of me as a pest. Nina's father was a good man, but he was very strict. When 9:30 p.m. came, any boys who were around his home had better be hitting the road. He would let people know it was time to leave by clearing his throat or throwing his shoe across the floor. He did not have to do that twice.

When I first starting dating Nina, my means of travel was a bicycle. It was not always easy to get to her home by bicycle. Nina's brother had a dog named Rattler, and he had a special dislike for me. Somehow, he knew when I was coming and would be waiting behind the smokehouse. As I passed by the building, he would grab my leg. Oh, how I wanted to kill that dog, but I was afraid of Nina's dad.

Can you imagine a young fellow leaving his girl's house at 9:30 p.m. in this day? You cannot imagine a boy and girl being at the house at 9:30 p.m. At the time, I resented the strictness of Nina's dad, but as I look back, I am glad that he had rules because he loved his daughter and wanted the best for her.

It did not take me long to realize that I had fallen in love with Nina. I praise the Lord that she had fallen in love with me also. Neither of us, at that time, had any idea of what God had in store for our lives.

Before Nina and I got too serious with each other, I asked her about her relationship to Jesus Christ. Although she was not as active in church as I, she assured me that she was a Christian. This is so vital to every marriage. Every young Christian should be sure that the person he or she marries is a dedicated Christian. The fact that Nina and I started our lives together with Christ as the center has made all the difference in the world to us.

For a young man, 18 is very young for marriage. However, most young men in 1953 knew how to care for a family. I had been working for some months and already knew what it meant to buy groceries for the family. To be sure, the responsibilities did not stop with buying groceries.

I know, without a shadow of a doubt, that the Lord brought Nina and me together. When Nina agreed to marry me, I wanted to give her an engagement ring, but she was afraid of her father. This meant that we were going to elope. Neither Nina nor I would suggest this for any young couple. You miss much of the beauty of a planned wedding and you cause many people to be angry.

It was February 25, 1953. The day was cold and rainy as I went by and told my boss that I would not be in for work that day. I did not tell him the reason because Nina's brother worked with me. He would have gone to his father and probably would have stopped the wedding for a time. I was so afraid that Mr. Hood, Nina's father, would find out that we were getting married that I had three cars for the wedding. I knew that my car would be recognized so I borrowed my uncle's car. In the meantime, a good friend of mine used his car to take us to the courthouse.

There are those who feel that a person is not properly married if a minister does not do it. Nina and I both urge young people to be married by a minister. This gives them the opportunity to have proper counseling before marriage. As to the legality of our marriage, we have no doubts at all. On that cold February day, Nina met me at a friend's home just across the road from her home. To keep Nina's people from knowing what was happening, I wore a yellow shirt over my suit. When I saw Nina that day, my eyes sparked because she was so beautiful in her dress of blue. She and I were very afraid. Just as we left the house, we met her father and our hearts almost stopped, but he did not know what was happening. The service was at 2:00 at the courthouse. I will always remember how the secretaries strained their necks to see me kiss Nina. They were disappointed because I forgot to kiss her. I know what you are saying. "Boy, he sure was too young to get married." We did many things that day which probably seemed strange.

After the wedding, we went back to mother's house. We stayed with mother for about a month before we found a house to rent. We had supper with mother, grandmother, my uncle and some friends After supper we went to prayer meeting. Can you imagine going to church on your wedding night? I am glad that we did because we wanted Christ to be first in our lives. On the way to church, I ran over a rabbit. We took it home and Nina helped clean it. By now, you are probably saying we were really crazy. I had married a girl who knew how to take care of a home. She did not have to learn about the care of a home; she already knew. When we arrived at church, mother told the preacher that we had married, and he said, "Now you have two babies." I did not especially appreciate the remark.

There are many things that happened on our wedding day that Nina and I would like to have done differently. We would have liked for Nina's family to be at the wedding. This is especially true of her father. We would have loved for the wedding to be performed by a minister. It would have been great to be able to go on a honeymoon. This was not possible because I did not have the money, and I had to be back on the job the next day. I do not regret going to church on my wedding night. The difficulties we faced on our wedding day drew us closer together and helped prepare us for the many difficult, but happy, days ahead. My boss gave me my check on the weekend and said, "You are going to need this."

Chapter 8
Our First Home Together

It is the desire of every young couple to have a home of their own, or, at least, to be able to rent. When you are making $32 per week, you are not in a position to give your wife a large brick home. In fact, with a salary like that, you would not be able to build a log cabin. It is great to know that the Lord looks out for His own. My family lived close to an area known as "Honeymoon Hill." This particular hill was owned by the lady who was my first-grade teacher in school. When young couples in our area got married, they tried to get one of those cabins. When I got married, they were all occupied. Mrs. Rogers had her furniture in the end cabin. No one had been able to rent that cabin in the past. It was a long shot, but I decided to ask the dear lady about renting her cabin. She was kind enough to move her furniture into a barn and let me rent her cabin for $15 per month. Nina and I were elated. Nina, from the time that she was a little girl, was an excellent housekeeper. I have never had to worry about coming home to a dirty house or not having a fine home-cooked meal. This is a particular gift that she has, and I praise the Lord for it. We had to get some new furniture when we moved in, and she put me to work getting the windows and ceiling fixed. The cabin had one room and a kitchen. The main room had about 15 small windows. We took cardboard and covered the ceiling. It was not much, but it was a blessing to us. It was our first home together, and we were happy in the Lord. By this time, Nina's father had gotten over the anger of my stealing his baby daughter. It was a proud moment for us when he visited our home.

Soon after we moved into our home, my job ended. I was able to draw a little unemployment compensation. This bought food and paid the rent. During the winter and spring of 1953, jobs were rather hard to find. Although some people may have felt that we were lazy, a number of us men who were out of work, passed the time away by practicing baseball during the day and playing games at night. Robert Ray lived right by me, and we walked the mile together twice a day to the local store where the baseball players would meet. My wife finally got tired of my continual travels to the store and wished that I would leave the seat of my pants at the store. Sure enough, that is exactly what happened. Somehow, a nail found its way to my special chair. Although I was embarrassed, my wife was delighted that her wish had come true.

Later on, that summer, a number of us men were able to get a job in Columbia, South Carolina. It was a long distance to drive for $.80 per hour, but it was better than nothing. When a person does not have any particular skill, he has to accept what he can get. It was a tough job pushing a wheelbarrow filled with mixed cement. If a person were not mighty careful, the wheelbarrow would overpower him. The Lord was preparing me for tough days ahead. While I was working in Columbia, I found out that a bus driver was needed for the Dalzell Elementary School. I hesitated to take this job because Dalzell was being kept open when the officials of the school district knew that it was unethical. All the high school students had been transferred to other white schools.

After I talked with some of the parents who had children at Dalzell, I decided to take the job. My salary for driving the bus was $100 per month with an added $25 for working in the lunchroom. Things went along very well until I lost my driver's license. Prior to my beginning with the bus, I had an automobile accident and did not have liability insurance. Insurance was not mandatory at the time. However, I was still liable since the accident was my fault. The gentleman, whom I hit, was very kind and did not press charges against me. Since I was unemployed at the time of the accident,

I could not pay for the damages to his car. Because of this, the Highway Department suspended my driver's license. I was deeply disappointed because my wife and I were just beginning to see our way clear. We were also expecting our first child. The County Superintendent of Schools tried to get the Highway Department to give me a license to drive the bus, but the Highway Department refused. I sought help from a local attorney who informed me that he could do nothing until a year had passed. When the liability insurance law was passed in South Carolina, a clause, which had been inserted, stated that a license would have to be granted if this was a person's means of earning a living. I took this clause and headed for the main Highway Department in Columbia. When I arrived and stated my problem, the man in charge said, "I am sorry, but we have a boy in Sumter with the same problem, and there is nothing we can do." I let him know that I was that boy and handed him the clause with reference to the license. He read the paper and said to his secretary, "Write him out a driver's license." It is not always easy to understand why things happen, and many times, we will never know why, but God has a marvelous way of working out things that seem tragic. God was showing us again that He would take care of the difficult things. By the beginning of 1954, I was driving the bus again. This was a blessing because our first son was born March 1, 1954. Clayton brought joy to our home, and Nina and I were determined to bring him up under the leadership of our Lord. The Lord had given him to us, and it was our desire that he be used of the Lord.

Chapter 9
A Classroom in a Bus

Since I had extra time on my hands as a bus driver, I decided to take an English course through correspondence. That was one of the best decisions that I had made in a long time. My uncle, who was better trained than I, would continually correct me when I used my words incorrectly. He did the correcting for my good, but my blood pressure would still boil. The English course helped me with my speaking and writing abilities. God was preparing me for the ministry, and I did not realize it. His plan was being worked out. Many people have the idea that things just happen by chance, but the child of God knows that the Lord is in control of things. I do not understand all that Paul is talking about in the eighth chapter of Romans, but I do believe that God had, and still has, a plan for His children. The Lord is all-powerful, and even though He gives us free will, we must realize that without Him, we cannot survive.

    The school bus was not only a place for the study of English, but I learned to read and study the Bible more effectively. The Bible helped me with the difficulties that I encountered. Although I was not much older than many of the students, I learned to face frustration and anger. If you do not already know it, I will assure you that a group of eighth graders can cause frustration and anger. While at the school, I had to be a ball player and a fighter. One young man chose me as a means to show the girls how strong he was. He tried his best to whip me at wrestling. To be perfectly honest with you, he came very close. Frustration really began to set in when my bus developed carburetor trouble. The bus would wait, it seemed to me, until I had passed all areas of help to give me trouble. It finally started to pop and skip and just finally died. The mechanic came and got me started but it was not long before the same thing happened again. After some investigation, it was found that the boys at the school had put grass and dirt in the gas tank. God was preparing me then for the eighth-grade class that I would teach some thirteen years later.

Long Branch Baptist Church called its first full-time pastor while I was driving the bus. Since I had some spare time, I agreed to take the pastor around to visit all the homes in the community. Little did I know at the time that God was preparing me for the pastorate. The pastor, Brother Burgess, was a tremendous help and a source of encouragement to me. I drove the bus for another year, and I do not suppose I will ever know how much that period of time moulded my life for work that the Lord was preparing me to enter. My life had touched others, but others had touched my life in ways that I never knew. I just hope that my life as a Christian, during those days at Dalzell, pointed someone to the Lord.

Chapter 10
Preparation in the Church

Many people touched my life as they witnessed to me about Jesus Christ. My family, led by the dedication and concern of my mother, had a profound effect upon my life. Most of the encouragement from my family came after I had accepted Jesus Christ as my Lord and Master.

When I accepted Jesus as my Lord, Long Branch Baptist Church did not have a full-time pastor. Because of this, different lay people in the church would conduct prayer meetings and visit with the teams in homes. Here was God's way of preparing me for the future. My uncle, Woodrow, had a public address system that we used for witnessing. He and his brother, Robert, would take me with them to the little towns of Pinewood, Elliot and Rembert. Woodrow would get power for the set from his car battery. He would play records and then each of us would give our testimony as to what Christ meant to our lives. The people around the stores would gather and listen to the songs and stories about Jesus. It was a wonderful way to share the Good News of our Lord. At the age of twenty, I was teaching the adult Sunday school class at Long Branch. Classes in the 50s were not departmentalized as they are today. Any adult, both men and women, made up that class. The average in the class was about 55. This was God's classroom where He was preparing me to preach the Gospel.

When I was 21 years old, I was asked to serve as a deacon of the Long Branch Baptist Church. God wanted me to serve with learned and tried men like Mr. Henry Benenhaley and others who had tremendous insights that they could share with me. It was a joy for me, as a young man, to have Brother Henry, who was the chairman of the deacons, come and talk with me about particular needs or problems of the church. God was giving me business as well as spiritual training which is needed in leading a church. God was moulding His clay for further use along the way. Little did I dream that one day I would return as pastor of the Long Branch Baptist Church.

Although I did not understand fully all that God was doing in my life, more and more He began to reveal to me that I was being called to be a pastor. This was very frightening to me because I was so unprepared educationally. All of this just proves that God is in control. Back in 1954, I never dreamed that God was opening doors of service in order to prepare me for future days. Things would be so much more peaceful if every Christian could really believe that God will work His purpose out through his life. Let me tell you, I have not arrived fully in this trusting completely without fear. Even though God has blessed me during all these years, I still have my doubts and fears, but I realize also that He still loves and cares for me. Finally, in June of 1955, I was licensed to preach. My pastor, Brother Doyle Burgess, was very helpful and understanding as he prayerfully guided me in those days of important decisions. My first sermon was really a big hit with some of the young people. To be honest, some stated that I should be the pastor. Their reason was that my sermon lasted five minutes. My text was taken from Galatians 6:7-8 KJV.

Nina was very understanding through all of this. This was new to her. She had been very faithful and supportive of me in all my teaching and visiting at Long Branch. We would walk the two miles from our home three times a week to church. I shall never forget the first Sunday we took our little boy, Clayton, to church. It was a cold day in March, but Nina carried him all the way. It was not that I was lazy and did not want to help; she just did not trust me to carry him. I thought sure she would smother the little fellow. Those were hard days and yet, they were glorious days. Through it all, our blessed Lord was moulding His clay. He did not love us more than others, but He had a special task for us to do. He was able to take unworthy clay and shape it according to His purpose. This is not to say that we did not fail Him, but we can say that He never failed us. There were many times when Nina and I grew frustrated, and our faith wavered, but He always gave us strength to continue.

From 1955 to 1958, God taught me a lesson in faith and patience. I am sure that this was true of Nina also. She never complained, but it must have been rough on her not knowing when she would have to pick up and move. Neither of us had ever been far from home. Before we got married, Nina had not been really active in church. This was partly because she had no way to attend. When she surrendered her all to the Lord, she did not hold back.

Chapter 11
Preparation for School

If I were going to be an effective minister, it would be necessary for me to further my education. Brother Burgess felt that I might be able to attend North Greenville Junior College. There were a number of factories in Greenville where I might be able to get a job in order to care for my family. Since I did not complete high school, North Greenville seemed to be the place for me to attend because they had a preparatory course to prepare students for college. Brother Burgess and his wife took Nina and me to Greenville on a very hot Saturday in 1955. The president of the school was very kind and let us know what would have to be done in order to attend school. He felt that I could attend North Greenville providing I got a job. Greenville was about nineteen miles from the college. This meant that I would have to attend classes during the day and work at night. This was a tall order for a person who was a good student. My grades at Edmunds High School were anything but good. Consequently, this trip to Greenville was very encouraging. God was still providing strength along the way.

    The big problem now was to get a job in Greenville. Brother Burgess introduced me to a friend who pastored a church in the same association where he served. This pastor had attended North Greenville and worked in a factory in Greenville. He agreed to take me to the factory where he worked and see if he could help me get a job. We ran into difficulty the first day in Greenville. We left home with the idea that we could be back by night. We just could not see the leaders at the factory and get back home that night. I would not be able to take the aptitude and physical tests until the next day.

Our next problem would be a place to stay. Brother Reid had a sister who let us spend the night at her home. Brother Reid called home and let our families know we would not be back until the next day. His sister was very gracious. Although she had to leave early the next morning to get to her job, she told us we could prepare breakfast when we got up. It sure is a good thing that Brother Reid could cook. I am not the world's best at such things.

The next day was beautiful, and I went to the factory in Greenville with expectancy. First, I took some tests to measure general mental ability and did OK. The physical seemed routine, and I felt good about the job. There was an opening if I qualified. When the nurse gave me the results of the physical, it seemed as if my world had caved in on me. I was hurt and frustrated. She said, "I am sorry, but your eyesight is not good enough for you to work around the machines in our factory." I knew that my right eye had poor vision, but I never dreamed that it would keep me from getting the job. "Why had God let me down?" This would be the normal reaction by some, and I must admit that I was thoroughly confused. Surely, I had not misunderstood the call of God, and yet, it seemed that I had. If I had not, why was the door closed? It would be almost two years before I knew the answer to that question. So many times, we blame God for closing doors when He always knows best. When I returned home, I was embarrassed to face people. My Sunday school class had already given us a going-away shower. Brother Burgess, being the wise pastor that he was, asked me to bring the message on Sunday. He understood the hurt and frustration that I was going through. He also knew that God had called me to preach. I trust that I will always be sensitive to the needs of others. Had this man of God not come to my rescue, it is very possible that I could have let disappointment keep me from following the will of my Lord. The members of Long Branch were very kind and understanding. I continued my work at the church and grew in the knowledge of my Lord.

Someone has said, "Hard work never killed anyone." That statement could be challenged, but hard work did not kill me. After the 1955 school year ended, I got a job with a local concrete company. When I went to work the first morning, I had a very good pair of leather gloves, but by afternoon, they were filled with holes. When you handle eight-inch blocks all day, it does not take the blocks long to cut through whatever one is wearing on his hands. If a person did not wear gloves, you can imagine what would have happened to his hands. I had been hired as a forklift operator but did whatever needed to be done. The work was hard, but again, God was preparing me for difficult days ahead. That first afternoon on the job, we had to unload a car box filled with bagged cement. This was in July, and the bags weighed from 90 to 100 pounds. When I got home that afternoon, I tried to get a drink of water, and the dipper dropped from my hands and slid across the floor. I was so tired that it was difficult for me to get a grip on the dipper. For those of you who do not know what a dipper is, it is used for everyone to drink from the bucket of water. We have become civilized now and do not use such things. In order to get to work each day, I had to catch the Greyhound bus. After work in the evenings, I was ashamed to get on the bus because I was so dirty. After a few months, I was able to buy a 1937 Chevrolet and drive it to work.

It is amazing how God can teach His children lessons. He did teach me a lesson about tithing through a 1942 Chevrolet car. I took the motor out of the 1937 Chevy and put it in the 1942 Chevy frame. This car had booster brakes and a vacuum shift transmission. During this time, I decided that I was too poor to tithe. Some people are too rich, but I was too poor. My salary was $32 per week. There was no way that I could give $3.20 to the church. God took care of that idea. Just about every week, that old car cost me over that amount. You might say that God did not have anything to do with it, but I think that He did. I have been tithing since then. The last time the '42 Chevrolet broke down, I sold it on the spot for $15 on credit. That car acted as if it was demon-possessed. My wife declares that she wore the end out of her housecoat pushing that old car every morning before I could go to work. One morning a friend pushed the old car with his for over a mile, and when it would not start, we found that it was out of gas. Something had happened to the fuel system, and the car was getting about five miles per gallon.

The job at the concrete company taught me a number of things: (1) It taught me the importance of being faithful with what I had, even though I felt capable of doing better; (2) There was the opportunity of being a witness for my Lord; (3) I was not alone in my plight; (4) Some lasting friendships were established. Some of the trucks we drove were out of the junkyard. I remember a particular day when I let praise go to my head. It fell my lot to take a load of blocks to a new church building downtown. I had to twist and turn that old truck every way but loose to get the blocks to the desired place. Finally, after much struggle, I succeeded. One of the construction workers came over and said, "That was some of the best driving I have ever seen." When I started out, the backend of the truck caught a stack of blocks and tore them to pieces. Needless to say, my boss was not at all pleased when I got back to the shop.

    When a person does his best on the job, even if that job is poor compared to others, a person will find something better. One afternoon after I got home from work, a friend of mine came and told me where I could find a new job. It was with a local furniture company in town. Since the company was working about 60 hours per week, my salary would almost double, and there would be insurance benefits. I took the job and the Lord really blessed me.

    After I started the new job, I realized that I needed a better car in order to get to work. Money was not easy to get because I did not have any credit at the bank. An uncle of mine suggested that I ask Mr. Henry Benenhaley to loan me the money. Brother Henry and I were deacons at the same church, but I was hesitant about asking him to loan me the money. Finally, I got up enough nerve and went to see what he would say. He informed me that he did not have the $300 cash, but he would sign a note at the bank for me. When I got to the bank on Monday, Brother Henry had the papers ready for me to sign. He even went to a local company to help me get a car. When I got to the Chevrolet Company, they had sold the car I wanted. They had a clean 1947 Ford that past Friday for $300. God had a hand in this because my uncle took me to Columbia the next Saturday, and I bought a very good car for $175. This left enough money for me to start a bank account. To me, this proves again that God has a plan for our lives and works things out according to His purpose.

    Every person, if he is honest, needs to search continually for improvements. Two years had passed since my disappointment of not getting a job in Greenville to continue my education. Some of my friends suggested that we attend the Opportunity School in Columbia two nights per week. I attended this same school a few weeks as a young person. I worked all day in Sumter and drove two nights a week to Columbia to attend classes. The courses in English were very helpful. One friend was delighted when he learned to write his name. This taught me a valuable lesson. Many times, we are not satisfied with what we have and yet there are others who would give anything to be able to have what we have educationally.

Things went very well on my job until I was told that we were going out on strike. We were going to ask for a $.05 raise per hour. It is hard to realize that people would get so upset about $.05. We walked a picket line and almost were thrown in jail. One of my fellow workers told an officer that he would like to see what the inside of a jail looked like. That might have been his desire, but it surely was not mine. You should have seen me getting him back on the other side of the road.

When our group went out on strike, I was drawing about $40 per week. While walking the picket lines, the union gave me $9 per week to buy groceries. I learned during that time not to let someone else do my thinking for me again. We went back to work without getting the $.05 raise and almost lost our jobs. The company did not treat us fairly, but we made a mistake in letting people lead us who did not know what they were doing. It was good to get back to work because those three weeks put me behind with my bills.

Chapter 12
A Place Prepared by God

While reading the Southern Baptist Home Mission Magazine one day, I found out why God had closed the door for me at North Greenville. The magazine told of a school where men could work and prepare themselves for the ministry. This was the Clear Creek Baptist School in Pineville, Kentucky. When I wrote the president and explained my situation to him, he wrote me a beautiful letter, letting me know that my prayers had been answered. A first-year student was required to attend classes in the mornings and work on the outside work program in the afternoon, according to his family's needs. My wife and I knew that God had opened the door. When I told my foreman that I was leaving for school, he wished me well and told me that my job would be waiting should I need to come back to Sumter. I appreciated his kindness very much. He has since passed away, but I praise the Lord that he accepted Jesus Christ as his Lord before he died.

There was an empty feeling in my stomach on that August day in 1958 when my family and I prepared to leave for Kentucky. My mother and grandmother were on the porch when we started to drive away. Wilbur, our second son, was eleven months old. My grandmother never could understand why I took her boys away. It was not that she was not a Christian. She was a dear saint of God, but she did not understand my need for further training. We were sad, but we had to go because it was God's will for our lives. There is a peace in doing the Lord's will, but it does not necessarily mean that a person is always happy.

When the deacons of the Long Branch Baptist Church found out that we were really moving to Kentucky, they asked the church to help with our moving expenses. The church agreed and along with what my uncle, Robert Hood, gave, we were able to pay the moving expenses. It just so happened that a moving company had just enough room for our small amount of furniture. It just happened that the truck had to go through Pineville, Kentucky. No, it did not just happen. God was in control. We sent our furniture ahead of us. We had no idea of what the school or Kentucky looked like. Many people probably thought of us as being foolish, but as things worked out, I believe it was God's directing.

The trip to Kentucky was hard. Our old '46 Ford did very well on the road. With our stops to care for the baby and eat lunch, it took us about 11 hours to travel the 350 miles. Boy, what roads. I had never seen such crooked roads. After we traveled through Asheville, North Carolina, it appeared that we were traveling in circles. Road 25 E through Tennessee looked like a snake. My wife and I were getting an education even before we started school. The worst was yet to come. When we got to Pineville, Kentucky, I missed the turn off to Clear Creek. I got on the mountain road that led up to Pine Mountain State Park, and a sign in front of me read, "Keep coming, you are not lost." If that sign could have understood, the words would have read differently. Nina and the boys were very brave through it all, but it must have been a very traumatic time for them. Finally, we got on the right road and found our way to Clear Creek. We stopped at the school store and bought some "preacher's steak" for supper. For you unenlightened people, that is bologna. By the time we reached our home, we were already homesick. We knew then why God had let us send our furniture ahead. If we had visited Clear Creek before we sent our furniture, it is very doubtful that we would have stayed. Everything was just so different from what we had been used to. We could not return home because we had spent our money. God never tricks us, but He knows how to handle us. That is good because He knows much better than we about what our limitations are. He knew we could get used to the mountains and even learn to love them. We sure did not know that at that particular time.

The movers had just placed our furniture in the middle of the house because they did not know in which rooms to place it. This was very discouraging because we were already tired. Nina was sick with a terrible sore throat, and this, in addition to her homesickness, did not help matters. By the time we got our furniture partly placed, we were ready for a good night's sleep. Sleep did not come easily because the creek right behind our house sounded as if it would come through the bedroom. To make matters worse, the railroad track was right by the house. It had been a difficult day, and because of the things that surrounded us that night, we were still in for a difficult time. But God had not let us down, and in the days ahead, we were to see His continual guidance in our lives. As I look back now, I praise Him for His loving guidance in each of our lives.

It did not take us long to find some gracious friends at the school. There were others who were just as lonely as we were. We found strength from those who had been at the school for a period of time. The school officials were super. Brother Aldridge was a man who was deeply concerned about people and their needs. Brother and Mrs. Moore were to have a profound effect upon the lives of my family. Brother John Holloway and his wife, along with Brother and Mrs. Arnold Moon, helped us. There were many other families who touched our lives.

Chapter 13
Hard at Work

It did not take me long to find that there was plenty of work to do. My first job found me working in the new furniture factory as a carpenter's helper. Brother Hermon Moore was the superintendent of buildings and grounds and he could get the work done. At first, I thought he was a real hard-nose boss, but as I worked with him, I found that he was a very fine boss and a good friend.

It was not going to be easy working part-time and just making $.75 per hour. God knew the needs of my family, and He worked things out for us. Brother Moore soon learned that I had done some plumbing work. He came and told me that his plumber was graduating, and he wanted me to take his place. This was a hard and dirty job, but it meant that I would work more hours. This meant more money. Since I was to do the plumbing work, the water treatment plant came under my job. This would mean two extra hours a day. Each day, I had to check the water plant and see that the proper amount of chemicals was added to the water to keep it pure. God was showing me, again, that he had called me for a special purpose, and He would see that our needs were met.

Plumbing work at Clear Creek provided all the excitement I needed. When someone's drain line became clogged, he called me. Had you suddenly walked upon me during one of my typical workdays, you would have thought that I was the grease monkey of the school. My clothes were smeared with pipe dope and oil, and I really looked like a fellow who was ready for the poor house. When I crawled under the cottages, I had to be on guard against snakes, scorpions, and most of all, the rumble of water after a commode had been flushed. It was a helpless feeling to be flat on your back, unable to move, and hear a commode flush. This was especially true, when you were right under a broken line. Sure, we asked the people not to flush the commodes while we were working, but have you ever gotten all Baptists to follow rules?

My most trying times would come just before dinner when I would have to turn off the gas on campus because of a broken line. You can imagine the anger of the wives who were trying to get dinner for their husbands in order for them to get to class on time. When I would get the line fixed, many of the wives would want me to come and light their stoves and hot water heaters for them. Since my wife had learned to light ours, she finally lost her patience and told the women to light their own. It did not take them long to get the message. My wife did what I wanted to do all along.

Work at Cedar Creek had to be done at all hours of the day and night. One cold morning, Brother Moore knocked on my door at 4:00 a.m. in the morning. He informed me that the water was off all over the campus. We began looking for the cause and soon realized that we were in for a long hard day, or even days. I do not have any idea of the number of trips I made up the mountain from the water treatment plant to the storage tank. We just could not locate the cause of the problem. We removed all the sand and gravel from the treatment tank thinking that there might be a leak there. We worked all day and late into the night without any luck of finding the cause. Another crew worked all day Sunday and still did not find the answer. It was a good thing that we had an emergency system for water. Finally, on Monday, the broken line was found high up on a mountainside. There were no roads or paths up the mountainside, and to make matters worse, there was snow on the mountain. My crew and I had to carry pipe and equipment up that mountain to fix the break. It was not easy to cut and thread a six-inch pipe in such an area. After much struggle, we finished the job and really felt a sense of pride as the campus, once again, had its full water supply.

There were times at Clear Creek, had I not known that God had called me to preach, that I would have left. This was not a feeling that was unique to me. I am sure that many of the other men felt the same way. I did work at Clear Creek that I probably would not have done anywhere else. It is not easy to clean a septic tank with buckets, but I did it at Clear Creek. Had Brother Moore told me to do this while he watched, I probably would have refused. But you see, he helped me clean the tanks. I never shall forget the time when we had to dig all the gas lines up leading to Bear Trail. This trail was steep, and we had to use metal detectors to find the pipes. We did this type of work in the summer and winter, but God gave us the strength to keep going. I do not know that I ever worked harder anywhere else, but I thank God for the work and opportunities that were provided at Clear Creek.

Clear Creek had two work programs for students. First-year students worked on the outside program while second-year students worked in the furniture factory. A policy stated that a second-year student would automatically go to the factory to work. Because of my experience, the school officials wanted me to stay with the outside work program. Although the work was easier, I probably would not make as much in the factory as I did on the outside. Under the present rules, the school officials could not give me a raise to keep me in my present job. The two groups got together and worked out a compromise. I was given a straight salary and put in charge of the work details under Brother Moore. God sure does know how to take care of His children. My salary was $35 per week. If I had to be out because of sickness or went home during Christmas or summer, my pay was still the same.

There was humor, at times, on the job. One student called me a "poor straw boss" one day when I had not received the work orders for the day. I assured him that I would put him to digging a ditch just as soon as I got the orders. After that, he was careful not to call me a "straw boss."

Chapter 14
Opportunities for Service in the Mountains

A number of Clear Creek students joined the Hosman Baptist Church at Tinsley, Kentucky. This was a small, but very friendly church. I learned some valuable lessons at this church. One of the good members of the church informed all the students from Clear Creek that he wanted to fill all our gas cans, so we could attend all of the services. Being a good South Carolinian, I informed him that I had enough money to buy my gas. I would not have had it if it had not been for my uncle, Robert Hood. The dear member said to me, "Son, you are new in the mountains, and let me tell you something. If a person here offers you something, do not turn it down because he will not offer it to you unless he wants you to have it." Brother, I learned my lesson very quickly.

Hosman sponsored a little mission near Harlan, Kentucky. This mission was about 20 miles from Clear Creek. I was asked to go over one Sunday afternoon and preach for the members of the mission. I shall never forget this experience. The road across the mountain was terrible. Just one car could travel the road at a time. There was no place to pass. If cars met on the road, one would have to back down the mountain until a place was found to pull off on the side. One side of the road was rocky and straight up, while the other side was open and straight down. Brother, you had to have faith to travel that road. It is no surprise that Clear Creek did not have any liberal students.

When time came for Hosman to select a pastor for the mission, I had no dream that I would be chosen. In fact, when my name was put before the church, I was shocked. One of the other students had been supplying at the mission, and I felt that he should have been asked. The student who had been supplying at the mission was disappointed and hurt. Maybe I should have turned the church down. I was young and did not know much about ethics at the time. It was my desire to do God's will, and I would not have done anything to hurt my brother for any amount of money. He let me know that he was disappointed, but he felt the church had made the right choice, especially since the mission asked for me without knowing that the church had selected me to go as pastor.

My family and I had some great experiences at that little mission. Those who attended were mostly women. We had one man who came. My family and I would have to leave Clear Creek very early on Sunday mornings in order to be on time. We met in a one-room school building with a big wooden stove in the middle of the room. My, it was cold until I could get the fire going. At first, the ladies would smoke in the building, but when I let them know that the building belonged to the Lord, they stopped. Our services were very informal, and the members seemed to be blessed by the Lord. The oldest member was truly a blessing to be around. Every Sunday during the invitation, she would shout the praises of her Lord. It was real with her. She did not disturb the services, but in her own way, she was very close to her Lord. My oldest son had never seen anyone shout before, so the first time this dear lady jumped up and shouted, he fell backwards in the floor. He was in no way making fun of her; he was just caught by surprise.

Many lessons in life are learned the hard way. I had never been used to driving on snow until I moved to Kentucky. One Sunday, when we got up, the ground was covered with snow. Travel had been light that morning, so my car moved through the snow very well. My family decided to stay home that morning, but I was sure that I could get to the mission. Traveling on the highway was fine, but when I got to the mountain area, things were quite different. When I tried to make it across the mountain, my car would just slide across the road. I turned around and started back home but could not make it. Many of the preachers, who had been just as crazy as I, had to stop at a little store at the bottom of the mountain. We were going to have to wait until the road plows cleared the road. This would not be until the afternoon. When the storeowner found out that we were preachers, he told us that his grandmother, who was sick, would be glad for us to hold services in her home. We were delighted and went to her home. We were in for another surprise. Many mountain preachers did not think very highly of Clear Creek students. It was their belief that God would give His man a message, and there was no need for schooling. When a local preacher found out that a meeting was being held in the grandmother's home, he decided to attend. I suppose he was coming to see if our theology was correct. I am not saying that the theology was correct, but the local preacher probably was not sure himself about correct theology. In some areas of the mountains, the preacher who preached first was in trouble because all those who followed would use the same text and see who could out-preach the other. This sounds very critical, but it is true. I am sure that things have changed some by now. Finally, that afternoon, we were able to get back home after the roads had been cleared. You can be sure that I did not travel those roads again just after a big snow.

As has already been stated, the mountain road to the mission was very bad. One night when we were having revival, the fuel pump stopped working on my car as we were going up the mountain road. There was no place to pull off the road. The cliff of rocks was on the driver's side and a complete drop off was on my wife's side. To make things worse, it was night. I had to let the car roll backwards down the mountainside. In order to do this, I opened my door and guided myself by staying as close as possible to the cliff on my side. My wife declares that she left her fingerprints on the dashboard. Although there were no brakes on her side, she pushed the floorboard just the same. God took care of us and let us come to safety at the bottom of the mountain. It was His way of letting us know that He was still guiding and working out His plan through our lives. We did not see any visible results of decisions during the meeting, but we knew that any true decisions must come because of the power of the Holy Spirit moving in the lives of the people.

Nina and I had been home during the Thanksgiving period because her dad had gotten sick. When Christmastime drew near, we wanted to return to South Carolina, but were not sure about getting someone to supply for us at the mission. A student friend agreed to supply, and we were able to go for the Christmas holidays with our families. This was a good time, and during those days together, we could realize how God was taking care of us, step-by-step. While we were home, Brother Doyle Burgess, who had been so supportive of my ministry, resigned as pastor of the Long Branch Baptist Church. This was a sad time, and yet, we felt that he was doing what he felt God was leading him to do.

My stay at the mission was a time of learning for me. The church gave us $25 per month to pastor the mission. Because of the rough road, my 1946 Ford was about to come apart. As I continued to go each Sunday morning to the little mission, I became discouraged because no one had been saved. During the summer, my preacher friend agreed to supply while we went home for a few days. When I returned, he informed me that a number of people had accepted Jesus as Lord. I should have rejoiced, but I asked myself how this could be. My friend talked really slowly and was not nearly as dynamic as I. You can see how the old devil causes us to be jealous and makes us believe that God's work is dependent on how loud one can talk. My Lord taught me a lesson that day, and I hope that I will never forget that God uses people who have various and different gifts.

Chapter 15
Leaving the Mission

After I had been at the mission for about six months, the opportunity came for me to move to a church that was closer to the school and would provide more opportunities for service. I have no doubt that it was God's will for me to take this new opportunity, but I made a mistake in the way I resigned from the mission. Instead of going back to the mission and letting the people know that I was leaving, I went to the church pastor who was sponsoring the mission and told him my plans. It was not my intention to overlook the people. I should have given my resignation to the mission and then informed the church. I am not making any excuse. I made a mistake, and it haunts me. I was overcome with the opportunity to serve a church with a full-time program. This church had 200 in Sunday School while the mission had 15. I would be paid $30 per week where I had been paid $25 per month. Even if there had been 2000 in Sunday School or $200 per week, I made a mistake in the way I left the mission. Technically, I went through the proper channels. It was the church which was paying me and had asked me to take the mission, but I should have gone back and explained to the people at the mission as to why I was leaving. Because of lack of experience, I was afraid that the church would get someone else to come and help them. Every young pastor should be concerned about people regardless of who they are. He should never use people for his own ends. It is not how large the church or the salary is, but rather, that one is in the will of his Lord.

The Riverside Baptist Church at Four Mile, Kentucky is the church I accepted when I left the mission. Riverside called me to help them during a time when their pastor was very ill. This church provided valuable experience in directing a church program. I learned the importance of proper sermon preparation. This church had been used to tremendous Biblical preaching for the past 14 years. Since I was in school, having to be responsible for two sermons on Sunday plus Wednesday prayer service was difficult. Being the bright student that I was, I decided that I would select an easy book of the Bible and teach it verse by verse on Wednesday nights. I chose the book of Hebrews. The first Wednesday night, I soon realized that Hebrews was not easy at all. The study was made more complicated by the pastor being there. He was a good Bible student, and this made me feel even more inadequate. Needless to say, I found that no book of the Bible is easy. There is no shortcut for study and preparation. Through all these times of frustration, God took care of me. He provided the necessary means for my family to be happy. Consequently, as a family, we grew in the knowledge of our Lord.

The people at Riverside were very gracious to my family and me. They made us feel right at home, and this took some of the homesickness away from us. Our first Christmas season as assistant pastor to the church was made very enjoyable by the kindness of the members. The men of the church bought me a new suit, and the ladies bought my wife a beautiful dress. The church also made it possible for us to spend Christmas with our family in South Carolina. When I entered the church on Sunday before we went home, one man put something in my pocket and stated that it would help us on our trip home. He also told me to get tires for my car and charge them to him. When I got back to school that night, I found that he had put a $20 bill in my pocket. This was enough money to buy gas for the trip home. The Lord had provided again, and we were grateful.

Chapter 16
Surprise at the Church

When I started preaching at Riverside Baptist Church, softball season had just begun, and I started playing for them. Before this, I had been playing for Hosman Baptist Church and was doing very well. Riverside had high hopes that I would help their team, but for some reason, I really went into a slump. We still had a very good time together.

By this time, my old '46 Ford had seen its best days. The mountain roads to the mission had taken their toll. One day, I decided to correct a problem that I was having with my fuel pump. The fuel pump on the old Ford could be packed with a piece of leather, and this would cause the gas to flow to the carburetor. If you needed work done on your car, you would not have wanted me. Evidently, I put too much leather in the pump, and as a result, something broke in the motor. I think one of the rings cracked or came off the piston. The car started using a tremendous amount of oil. When the men of the church heard about my problem, they suggested that I wait until I returned from South Carolina before I sought to fix the car. My car used ten quarts of oil from Kentucky to South Carolina and back. This was a round trip of 700 miles. You have heard the saying, "Check my gas and fill it with oil"; my situation was similar to that.

When I returned to Clear Creek after my summer vacation, I was expecting some of my men from the church to loan me the money to have my car fixed. My reasoning was because they asked me not to have it repaired until I returned from vacation. At our next ballgame, the men asked me to stop by Riverside Church for a little get-together. I tried to tell them that I was not dressed for church, and they assured me that it would be alright to come just as I was. When we arrived at the church, a number of members, along with the pastor, who was ill, were there. The pastor said to me, "Brother Benenhaley, I did not know that the church was going to be turned into a used car lot, but if you will give the men of the church your old car, they want you to have the one parked over there." One of the men had been driving the sharpest 1951 Ford that I had seen in a long time. It was mine, and I did not have any dreams of such a gift. The men of the church had gotten together at the local utility plant and took up money to buy the car. I did not know whether to shout or cry. My, the goodness of our Lord. You probably figured that I would not accept the gift. Remember, I learned my lesson when I first came to Kentucky when a dear friend of Hosman said, "If the people of Kentucky give you something, they want you to have it." My family and I accepted the car with thankful and grateful hearts. We knew that God was supplying our need. When I drove the car back to Clear Creek, I had to show it off to some of my student friends. The men bought the car, filled it up with gas and bought the license plate tag for it. Later that week, the carburetor started giving me trouble, and the men had a new one installed. God is so good, isn't He? He uses godly people to help others who are in need.

My experiences at Riverside were a time of learning for me. This was also true for my wife. My children were blessed by knowing the great people at the church. The beloved pastor of the church died of cancer. He had been with the church for 14 years. The church needed a full-time pastor, and a committee was chosen to find the right person. Some of the members wanted me as pastor, but the committee felt that the church needed a more experienced man. After some months, a good man came as the pastor. My experiences at Riverside were a blessing, and I am sure that they helped prepare me for my first full-time church.

Chapter 17
Supply Preaching

When I found out that Riverside was going to call another pastor, I went back to supply work in the area around Pineville and continued to work at Clear Creek. The Lord opened various doors of service for me on the weekends. I also had the opportunity to conduct a few revival meetings. If, in the mountains, some people stated that they enjoyed your little talk, you could be assured that you were not their "kind of preacher." There were times when I had this happen to me.

My wife and I went to Virginia one Sunday morning because of a call to a church. Oh, how it snowed that day. But being the dedicated preacher that I was, we slipped and slid to the church. My ego was not helped at all when just a few people showed up for my services. Since I had driven 15 miles to get to the church, I thought surely more people would have been there. In my opinion, they were not very concerned about getting a pastor, that is, those who stayed home. After the morning service and lunch, the chairman of the pulpit committee took my wife and me to see the parsonage. My wife and I got an education that day. The parsonage had a storage tank where rain water was caught to furnish water for the house. If a dry season came, a person might have gotten a little thirsty. The chairman of the pulpit committee asked me if I would be willing to come and preach on another Sunday. I declined because I felt that my family and I had done our part. You do a lot of things on the spur of the moment when you are young. This is not to say I am old now, but several days have passed since then.

Along with my preaching on the weekends, the workdays at Clear Creek were very interesting. It was not necessary to make many trips up to the water storage tank at Clear Creek. Since it was my job to keep the water purified when a problem did occur at the main plant, I would have to take the purifying chemicals up to the storage tank and pour them in manually. It just so happened that the main plant had a problem one very hot day, and it was my luck, along with another student worker, to have to carry the chemicals up the rugged mountainside. To make matters worse, the storage tank was surrounded by some very high weeds. If you know anything about the mountains, you know that a creature known as the copperhead snake loves weeds and rocky areas. This creature does not have any respect for anyone. He does not even like preachers who are Bible students. He is even worse than some Baptist members when it comes to taking wrath out on a preacher. My friend and I were very much aware of this creature as we made our way through the weeds. Just to be on the safe side, we broke some long sticks and beat the weeds down as we moved along. Suddenly, without warning, something jumped straight up in front of us as our sticks came down in the weeds. We did not stand around arguing as to whether it was a copperhead or not. I meant to run far enough to be out of reach, but my friend shoved me aside, and down the hill he went. He was going to be sure that he was well out of reach of that thing. I moved so fast that I lost my hat. We did not pour the chemicals into the tank. In fact, we left the containers right where we dropped them.

When Brother Moore heard about our snake adventure, he had a big laugh. He kept this in mind when I helped him gather the eggs at the chicken house sometime later. As he gathered the eggs, he motioned for me to get the eggs out of a certain nest. I should have known that something was wrong. When I stuck my hand in the nest, an old black snake came slithering out. I almost fainted and Brother Moore almost died laughing. He knew that thing was in the nest. From then on, he called me the "snake handler." The term, "snake handler" is well known in Kentucky. Some religious groups actually handle rattlesnakes in their services.

Chapter 18
Sad News from Home

When Nina and I left South Carolina, her father was not in good health. He had a heart condition that was further complicated by high blood pressure. Two months after we arrived at Clear Creek in August of 1958, we had to make arrangements to return home because Nina's father had gotten worse. For a time, he seemed to get a little better, but we were aware that anything could happen because of his age and physical condition.

    Nina was very concerned about the spiritual condition of her father. Although he was a very good father, he did not profess to be a Christian. In fact, he did not attend church very often. I knew that I should talk with him about his relationship to Jesus Christ, but I was actually afraid. This was the old devil's way of getting me to leave him alone. One night before we were to return to South Carolina in the summer, Nina and I got down on our knees by the bedside and prayed for the salvation of her father. She and I both wanted the strength to witness to him. We returned home that summer of 1960, determined to share Christ with him. He was not well when we got home, but he was able to be up and around. We needed an excuse to get him away from the house, so we asked him to ride to the store with us. On our way, Nina and I began to talk with him about the things of our Lord. We were overjoyed when he related to us that he had accepted Jesus Christ as his Lord. I was happy, and I knew that Nina was thrilled. Nina probably knew that she might never see her father alive again as we left for Kentucky, but she knew that she would see him in Heaven.

    It was an October night when a friend came to my door and informed me that I had a long-distance phone call. When I picked up the phone, I recognized the voice of the pastor of the Long Branch Baptist Church back home. He had tried to get me earlier, but we were at prayer meeting. He gave me the news that Nina's father had passed away. With a heavy heart, I returned home and broke the news to Nina. Naturally, she was hurt, but being the Christian that she was, she put it all in the hands of our Lord. Due to the pressure of getting the call and having to leave so early the next morning, Nina got up the next morning with a terrible headache. It was difficult for her to travel, but we made the trip safely. It was afternoon before we reached Nina's home. We greeted the family and tried to prepare for the hours ahead.

The many friends in the community made the sad occasion lighter by just being near and letting the family know that they cared. This is the marvelous thing about being a Christian. You cannot remove the hurt, but it is good to know that people care. The Long Branch community has long been known for the concern and help that it provides for those who are in need. Nina's father had lived to be in his 70s. He had not given much of his time to the Lord, but his recent acceptance of the Lord meant that he had a home in Heaven. What a Lord we have! We may forget Him, but He does not forget us. Mr. Hood took a tremendous chance by waiting so long before he accepted Christ, but thanks to the Lord for answering when he did call upon Him. Don't you know that this made it easier for his children as they followed him to the church and cemetery? "But I would not have you to be ignorant, brethren, concerning them which are asleep, that ye sorrow not, even as others which have no hope" (1 Thessalonians 4:13 KJV). This hope is like an ointment to a sore, a rock in a time of storm and a shield against the devil. Praise God for hope beyond the grave because of our Lord Jesus who won the victory over the grave. The funeral services for Nina's father were simple and helpful. The sermon by the pastor and the songs by the choir made things easier for the family. I pity people who never think about God and His church. What a tragedy when people laugh and criticize the church. The church is where comfort can be found in the day of trouble. It is the church member, born again, filled with the love of God who can say a word of comfort when you need it so desperately. While the old enemy Satan laughs at our hurts and sorrows, it is our Lord who draws us to Himself and says, "A man that hath friends must show himself friendly; and there is a friend that sticketh closer than a brother" (Proverbs 18:24 KJV).

Chapter 19
My First Full-time Church

My first experience with the Concord Baptist Church was during a weekend revival. The pastor, who was a teacher at Clear Creek, had invited me to conduct the meeting. We had a very good time together. It was during these services that my oldest son made a profession of faith in Jesus Christ. There were several other young people who made decisions during that weekend. It was not long after this when the pulpit committee approached me about accepting the church as pastor. After some time of thought and prayer, I informed the committee that I would be willing to accept the church until time for my graduation. After graduation, I wanted to enroll in college if the Lord opened the door. At the time, I did not feel that I would be able to attend college if I stayed at Concord. Little did I know that God was opening the door right then for me to attend college.

The chairman of the deacons of Concord brought his truck to move us. It was a busy time, but it was a time when my family and I knew that we were in the will of our Lord. There were many spiritual and physical needs at the church. The community needed to be visited and the building was in need of repairs.

Although Concord was the first full-time church I had pastored, the people really worked with me as though I were a seasoned veteran. No one treated me like a novice. I am sure the Lord blessed the church for that. Many churches want a young man, but they want him to have years of experience at the same time.

The first week on the field, I was called upon to conduct a funeral. God gave me the strength to conduct the service and minister to the family. I grew close to my members and they to me.

The Concord Baptist Church requested the Riverside Baptist Church to ordain me since I had been a member of that church. I believe this was the correct procedure to use. My home church had offered to ordain me. This was an honor, and I appreciated the fact that they would, but I felt that I should be called to a church before I was ordained. It is my belief that many men rob themselves of blessings by being ordained too early. When a man is ordained in the presence of the church which calls him, he gives that church the opportunity to participate and, also, the opportunity for them to learn more about him as a person and pastor. By being ordained in the area where one is to serve, he gives the church and pastors in that area the opportunity to know him better. Many men seek ordination before it is needed.

January 15, 1961 was a very special day in my life as I sat before the ordination council in the Riverside Baptist Church. My pastor led in the questioning, and pastors, deacons and teachers had an opportunity to ask questions about my call, Biblical beliefs and church views. The questioning was thorough, but it was done in a spirit of love and concern. I will always be thankful for the helpfulness of those men.

Chapter 20
Graduation Time

Getting ready for graduation was an exciting time. Although I was 25 years old, I had not even graduated from high school. This was a thrill that only God could understand. God had helped me reach a stage in my life that I was not sure was possible. When I left South Carolina to attend Clear Creek I was not sure that I could make grades which would be acceptable enough for me to stay in school.

When class officers were elected, I was chosen as the president of the senior class. We had a number of events leading up to graduation, which were very special. Our senior banquet supper was a very enjoyable time for all of us. Two of my young ladies from the church did without lunch in order to buy flowers for Nina and me for the banquet.

My mother and aunt came from South Carolina to be at my graduation. Mother had tried hard to provide the means whereby I could get an education, and I am sure this was a proud moment for her.

Graduation time finally came, and we gathered in the school chapel. My suit came from the thrift shop at school. It was new, but the color surely did not do anything for me. It was a light brown. After all the speeches were made, it came time for President Aldridge to give the President's Medal to the student who was chosen by the faculty as the one most likely to succeed. My wife and I were shocked when we were called to the front. President Aldridge stated that I never would have been able to get this medal had it not been for the faithfulness and dedication of my wife. Nina really should have been the one who received the award. I was humbled and thankful for the award. There were others who were just as deserving of the award.

That afternoon after graduation, I lost the medal. My wife and I searched all the areas of the house and even went back to Clear Creek to see if anyone had found it. I was embarrassed and ashamed to tell the president that I had lost the award. The next day, we found the medal lodged in the rubber of my car door. Evidently it lodged there when I started to get out of the car.

Chapter 21
Clear Creek's Impact upon My Life

Clear Creek made it possible for me to attend school and provide a living for my family. Things were surely difficult. We did not have the best of food to eat or clothes to wear, but we had enough, and we thanked our blessed Lord for providing for us. During those days, we stayed closer to our Lord because we learned how to depend upon Him. My wife tells a story which gives some idea about hard times at Clear Creek. A friend of ours said to her boys one night, "Boys, it's beans tonight or else." One of the boys thought for a moment and replied, "Mother, give me some of that 'else' because I am tired of beans." The people in Kentucky do love their beans.

We did not make much money, but we made enough to keep our families fed, clothed and warm. Many churches from throughout Kentucky and Tennessee brought good clothes, some new, to the thrift shop. The thrift shop was open on certain days, and you could find men and women searching for a particular size.

The fellowship at Clear Creek was great. Faculty, staff and students worked together beautifully. We learned from each other. We understood each other, and as a result, we grew as a Christian family.

In-service training at Clear Creek was very helpful. Students who did not pastor churches held services in the local jail. My first experience as a jail minister was rather revealing to me. I learned to appreciate and care for people more. My knowledge of dealing with problems, especially when talking with jail inmates, was increased. My experiences with the small churches in the area were very helpful. I learned to have a special empathy for people. When I first arrived at Clear Creek, I was told by a local preacher, just as some of the other preachers were, that I would not be able to pastor in the area because I was a "foreigner." This statement hurt and angered me because I thought the student was talking about my Turkish background. He was talking about anyone who was not a Kentuckian. His statements did not prove true because I was well accepted by the people in the area. My family and I really fell in love with the mountains, and especially the people. As I continued to supply and do revival preaching, I learned to be close to people in their times of need. God has given to me and my wife a deep concern for people. Many times, we have had to learn how to get away from problems in order to protect our own health. If we were not very careful, we would end up taking our problems, and those of others, to bed with us.

The Biblical teaching at Clear Creek was great. I learned more Bible there than at any other school. The courses dealing with Baptist doctrine were especially rewarding. When I entered Clear Creek, I was a Southern Baptist, but I was not really sure why. In fact, I had been saved while listening to a Nazarene pastor. My life also had been influenced by some radio preachers who were either interdenominational or independent. My courses in Baptist doctrine helped me understand the Biblical practices of Southern Baptists and helped me understand why I was a Southern Baptist. We studied the New Hampshire Confession of Faith, and with each doctrine we had to learn a number of scriptures to go along with that doctrine. Scripture memorization became a vital part of my study. For the final exam in Baptist doctrines, the requirements were to memorize 25 verses of scripture and four definitions. Each missed word in a verse counted off five points. I learned to memorize verses by writing them over and over again. This knowledge of scripture has added tremendously to my preaching ability. The studies at Clear Creek were great because the teachers believed and taught the Bible as the authoritative word of God. As a result, the student preachers preached with authority because they believed that they were delivering the message of God to the people. Statistics show that wherever Clear Creek students serve, evangelism and missions are encouraged and practiced. If a student left Clear Creek and did not have a thorough knowledge of the English Bible, it was his own fault. My days at Clear Creek prepared me for seminary. My knowledge of the Bible helped me grow stronger in the Lord when I faced different theological and philosophical theories. If a student is not very careful, he will substitute theory for fact. Many seminary professors are branded liberal just because students fail to distinguish between a theory and a fact.

Although I had to learn many things by trial and error, Clear Creek had taught me enough about the workings of a church so that I was able to get by very well when I was called to my first full-time church. The importance of the Association, State, and Southern Baptist Conventions had been drilled to us in many of our different courses. Because of that teaching and the importance of each to the local church, I have supported each and encouraged others to do the same. I am glad that I do not have to make a choice as to which school has been more important in my ministry. The Lord has been so precious in preparing the opportunity for me to study at different schools. Clear Creek just provided the opportunity for me to get the first training that was so essential to my entire ministry. Opportunity for ministry was opened that I never dreamed was possible. There were so many people who touched the lives of my family during this period, and I know it had to be the directing of our Lord. It was God's way of taking clay and moulding it according to His blessed will.

During my student days at Clear Creek, I met two students who were very strong in their beliefs about the doctrines of election and predestination. It was their belief that God called some to eternal punishment. I certainly did not agree with their teachings, but I did learn to have a greater respect for the sovereignty of God. God is all-powerful and all-knowing. He does direct our lives, and He has the right to demand obedience from us.

And we know that all things work together for good to them that love God, and to them who are called according to his purpose. For whom he did foreknow, he also did predestinate to be conformed to the image of his son, that he might be the firstborn among many brethren" (Romans 8:28-29 KJV).

These verses verify that God has a plan for His children. Many times, I forget that fact and must hang my head in shame. Too many times, I worry about things and forget that the Lord works problems out for His children. It is sad, but true, that many people miss the blessings of the Lord simply because people are not willing to make Him Lord of their lives. Yes, the Lord knows where His man should attend school, and He provides his needs. He knows what church a man should pastor and opens the door to the church.

Chapter 22
College-Bound

When I was first enrolled at Clear Creek, I had no dreams of college. At the time, I felt that my training at Clear Creek would be quite sufficient for the task which my Lord had called. My training at Clear Creek motivated me to seek more training at a college.

The president of Clear Creek suggested that I go and talk with the president of Cumberland College about the possibility of attending school there. Cumberland College is in Williamsburg, Kentucky. It is a Kentucky Baptist school that trains many school teachers for the mountainous areas. It would be difficult to attend college on my salary. The Concord Baptist Church was paying me $60 per week, plus a home and my utilities. But remember, I have already stated that God will take care of His own.

When I arrived at Cumberland College and went into the president's office, I found that Dr. Boswell was one of the finest men whom I had ever met. He knew of my needs by having talked with Brother Aldridge at Clear Creek. He assured me that he would do all that he could to help me get in school. It was not many weeks before I received a notice from his office stating that money had been provided for me to attend school.

When I accepted the pastorate of Concord Baptist Church, it was until I graduated from Clear Creek. Here again, I had failed to realize that the Lord had a long stay in mind. God knew that I would attend college at Cumberland and still minister to the people at the Concord Baptist Church. During the summer after graduation from Clear Creek, I had the opportunity to conduct a revival meeting in Marion, Indiana. During this time, my wife and I had the opportunity to think about staying at Concord. There was a problem because we really did not know whether the people wanted us to stay or not. I had had a good six months ministry at the church, but word had gotten back to me that a few older people did not like me because of my Turkish background. There are always those who do not like the preacher for one reason or another. My background was a reason for some. It must be said that it was a unique reason.

When I returned from Indiana, I explained to the leaders of the church about my opportunity to attend college. Up to this time, in the history of Concord, the church had always issued an annual call to their pastors. I explained to the church why I thought a pastor should be given an indefinite call. If God calls a man to a church, He should lead him away. Since God had opened the door to college, I felt that it was His will for me to stay at Concord. The church voted for me to stay as their pastor. Little did I know, at the time, that I would spend seven more years at Concord.

Registration day at Cumberland College was a frightening time for me. I did not know anyone, nor did I really know how to choose my subjects. I needed to get my classes organized in order to attend classes three days per week. Even then I would be traveling 240 miles per week. To get classes three times a week, I chose English composition and English literature. That was a bad mistake. I did not have much trouble with composition, but literature was a pain in the neck. Literature was really a second-year course. I was not prepared for the first year, much less the second. It was during my first year in college that I learned all about the dean's list. At the end of each semester, those who had a B average or better were placed on that list. He had another list for those who had less than a C average. Before the year was over, I had been on both.

During my first year at Cumberland, I rode to school with two preacher friends from Barbourville, Kentucky. This made the trips much easier on each of us as we took turns driving. The trips were used as a time of study back and forth to school. The two friends were studying Chaucer, and you would have thought you were in the old days of England, had you heard them.

Chapter 23
A Loving Church

Going to college and pastoring a church was not easy. Concord was limited in the amount of help they could provide. They knew the importance I had placed upon furthering my education. I think they shared my excitement. During times of excitement, it seems that many things can happen to dull that excitement. Just when things seemed to be all worked out for me to attend college, I found that the block had burst in my car. This meant a new motor or another car. My money was extremely limited, and I did not see how I could do either. When the deacons of Concord found out about the problem, they wanted to help. One of the deacons owned a car lot and informed the other deacons that he could let me have a car at a very good price. The deacons agreed that his offer was a good one and asked the church to buy the car for me. The church graciously voted to buy the car for me. I read often where a church buys a new car for their pastor or sends him on a special trip. Because of this fact, some people might ask, "What is so special about a church buying a used car for their pastor?" That time in my life was special because of the timing and the need. It was special because the people gave when they had needs of their own. It was special because I know that it was God's way of providing during the special need in our lives.

Pastoring Concord and attending college was a challenge, but it was also a happy time for my family and me. God blessed in a very special way. My family and I grew in the Lord as did the members of the church. During the first four years of my ministry at Concord, we averaged about 25 baptisms per year. This was not due to my great preaching or leadership; it was because the people got out and visited. The ladies of the church went into homes and told people about Jesus Christ. A deacon closed his place of business during certain hours in order to visit with me. We had revivals and at times would have to put chairs in the aisles. The church building, which was in need of repairs, began to take on a new look. New windows replaced old ones that fell in the floor when the wind blew hard. I remember well the excitement when we voted to put new pews in the church. Before this time, many of the members had not been tithing, and they probably thought that their young preacher was going crazy. In days gone by, churches would raise money by having bake sales, and people would actually collect money from people on the streets to help with certain projects. I informed our members that we were going to pay our bills without begging. When one man asked me how we would pay for the work being done at the church, I asked him, "Have you ever heard of tithing?" By the time we got the new pews in the church, the floors had been varnished, and most of the money for the work had been received. Many of the young people in the church worked hard, along with several of the other members, to get the job finished.

It was during these first years at Concord that my boys made a profession of faith in Jesus Christ. Clayton came during a weekend revival. He was among the first groups that I ever baptized. I had never baptized anyone before, and I wanted him to be first, but because there were some young ladies, I baptized them first. If I had it to do over, I think I would have baptized him first. It was later that Wilbur came by my study and told me that he wanted to be a Christian, like Clayton. I talked with him about his relationship to Jesus Christ and found that he did not fully understand what it meant to be a Christian. I explained to him that the blood of Jesus Christ would take care of him until he knew what it meant to accept Jesus Christ as Lord. He left my study crying; it was some time later before he came forward in the church and made a profession of faith. He assured me at this time that he knew what he was doing.

With children, we must be careful as we teach them the plan of salvation. How old should a person be, some will ask, before he accepts Jesus Christ as Lord? He certainly should be old enough to repent of his sins and realize that Jesus is the only way. He should be old enough to be following the leadership of the Holy Spirit rather than following someone who is a friend. Some children follow their friends down the aisle rather than being led by the Spirit. I would never tell a child that he is too young if he gives evidence of repentance and faith in the Lord Jesus Christ.

    I can well remember a little six-year-old girl who came one night at Concord and told me that she was accepting Jesus as Lord. She went back home that night and told her daddy what had happened. Her father was a sinful man. He drank and was unfaithful to his family. On the day that his daughter was to be baptized, he was drinking and had to leave the church before his daughter was baptized. One of the men of the church followed him outside and witnessed to him. The next morning that father was at my home and wanted to know if there was any work at the church that needed his help. He was a carpenter, so I let him work on the young married people's Sunday school class. This is the class he would be attending if he were coming to church. He did an excellent job with the class and even put the name of the class above the door. He started attending church and would sit in the very back. One night, during the invitation, he got up from his seat and made his way to the front, surrendering his life to the Lord Jesus Christ. The ladies of Concord had witnessed to him, and I am sure that the Lord used the witness of his six-year-old daughter to cause him to see his need of the Lord. I am glad that I did not tell that young girl that she was too young to accept Christ. It is very true that most six-year-old children would not understand what it means to trust Jesus as Lord. It is my firm belief that a person should understand what it means to accept Jesus as Lord before he or she is accepted as a candidate for baptism and church membership. Two years ago, when I went back to a homecoming at Concord, a young lady put her arms around my neck and thanked me for what I had said about her father. I had just made some remarks about a memorial in honor of her father who had died of a heart attack. This young lady had grown from a six-year-old to a beautiful wife and organist in the church. How wise and marvelous is our Lord!

Chapter 24
A Tremendous Loss

When time came for the second semester of college, I was down with the flu. I was very weak and the phone call letting us know that my grandmother had passed away did not help. One of the young men from Concord offered to drive me home for the funeral. I really did appreciate him for this because I do not think I could have driven home. This loss was extremely hard on me because I had spent the same amount of time with grandmother as I had with mother. I had been very close to her as a boy in South Carolina. Even after I married, I lived just a few houses away. As a boy in school, she would always have food warmed for me when I came home. I especially remember her having my hot chocolate warming by the fireplace. She loved her chickens and guineas. It was fun to look for the guinea nest along the ditch banks. Usually, by the time you were able to find a nest, it would be filled with eggs. Grandmother was a precious saint of God. She did not have any way of traveling until I was old enough to buy a car. She was delighted when I bought my first 1940 Mercury. This meant that she would be able to attend church and get around some of her friends occasionally. My grandmother dipped Railroad Mills snuff. Some will say that was one pleasure she had. I think it is very nasty, myself. After she surrendered to Jesus Christ, I told her she should not use snuff anymore. I felt that it was wrong as a Christian to use snuff. After I mentioned this to her, she never used snuff again. I still believe that it is wrong to use tobacco in any form. Some use the excuse that chewing or dipping is not as harmful as smoking, but I believe that any form of tobacco use hurts a Christian's witness. My grandmother did not get angry with me because she realized that her body was to be a temple of the Holy Spirit. After I heard of grandmother's death, I blamed myself to some extent because we had taken her visiting while we were home for Christmas. She developed pneumonia after we left, and I wondered if the trip out in the cold had contributed to her getting the disease. She had lived a long life and had blessed the lives of many.

Many friends made the loss of grandmother easier by their comforting words. I knew that mother was deeply hurt because she had cared for grandmother all those years and was with her when she died. In fact, she was alone with her when she passed away. During the funeral service, the sermon and music made things easier for all. I really do not know how people make it in times like those when they do not have the Lord to lean on for help. My grandmother had blessed my life, and as I left the cemetery, I knew that I had another reason for going to Heaven. The greatest reason of all is to see our Lord and thank Him for salvation, and it will be great to see those loved ones who have gone on before. The next time I started home and realized that I would not see grandmother, a sadness came over me that only the grace of God could remove. Now I know a little of what Nina must have gone through the first time she returned home after her father died.

After the funeral, I was able to return to school without losing any credit. The Lord worked through Dr. Boswell and others and my four years of schooling were provided.

Chapter 25
New Challenges during My College Days

During the summer, after my first year in college, our third son was born. Nina went to the hospital on Saturday morning, and Timothy was born that afternoon. Believe me, I learned to appreciate my wife and what a mother must go through to bring a child into the world. When Clayton was born, I sat near enough to the delivery room to hear my wife when the pain of delivery was intense. Wilbur was already born by the time I got to the hospital. This June day was different. The nurses let me stay in the room with my wife until just before delivery. I tried every trick to get out of that room, but Nina would not think of it. If children could only know how much their mothers suffered to bring them into the world, they surely would have more love and respect for them. A man who will turn his back upon his wife and children must be possessed by an evil spirit. Timothy was a small baby, but God blessed him with good health.

My college days presented many new opportunities both at college and in the church field. I was working on a combined major in history and political science with minors in English and sociology. Since I had gotten a good Biblical background at Clear Creek, I decided to try for a teacher's certificate. This area of study provided invaluable experiences for me. My teacher in the field of education was a man who took tremendous pride in what he was doing. He believed that a teacher should love and respect the students under his care. Many teachers refer, today, to their students as "kids." I believe that my director would have failed a student teacher who referred to his students as "kids." He informed us that "goats have kids." I looked forward to my student teaching days with fear and anticipation.

Lynn Camp High School, near Corbin, Kentucky was the school where I was assigned for my student teaching. My instructors taught history, Spanish and civics. I had two ninth grade classes of civics and one eleventh grade history class. My instructor had me put a Spanish test on the board; I did not know what I was writing down. I am glad that no student asked me a question about the test.

Both of my instructors were very helpful. At special times, the Director of Secondary Education from the college would come and observe my work. I was graded according to the way I dressed, the way I handled my students and the responses my students gave to my questions. If the students had so desired, they could have made me look terrible before my director. Sometimes, when the director was not at the school, I could not get my students to participate at all. Thanks to them and the Lord, it was different when the director came. My students made me look like a great teacher. They would answer as if they really enjoyed the studies. My students were just great. The director was impressed and gave me an A for the course. I felt like giving all my students an A, but I could not do that.

Those days at Lynn Camp prepared me for teaching later. It also helped me to understand the many different needs that people have. School teachers have a wonderful opportunity to help mould lives for useful living and service.

Teachers have a marvelous opportunity to be a witness by example and precept. It is true that Bible and prayer have been taken out of the school by many, but teachers can still be a witness for Jesus Christ. The courts have been blamed for the removal of Bible reading and prayer, but some people use this as an excuse not to do either. It is tragic that many teachers do not know how to read the Bible and pray.

May 1965 was another milestone in my life and that of my family. God was still moulding clay according to His divine plan. I was thirty years old when I graduated from college. Much that happened in those years would be considered routine by many. My mother and father separated before I was born, and some would say, "that happens every day." According to some, "It was just the bad breaks of life that a poor school was provided for the Turks." No, let's face facts; it is sin that breaks up a home, and it was sin that caused an inadequate school to be provided. It was because of wicked hearts that some people felt that they were better than others. But, somehow, God used the tragedies to give me the determination to prove that I could do better by the help of God and those who touched my life along the way.

My dropout record in school had seemed to place me among those who would never finish any type of schooling. Truthfully speaking, many of the disappointments along the way seemed to be a means of telling me that I would never make it. As I see it now, God used those difficult times to teach me patience (James 1:3 KJV). I have never fully understood Paul when he says, "And we know that all things work together for good to them that love God, to them who are called according to his purpose" (Romans 8:28 KJV). Yet God has taught me step by step that this is true. I was crushed that day when the nurse told me that I could not work in the factory because of my eyesight. I could not understand why God would let such a thing happen. Two years later, I understood when the Lord opened the door for me to attend Clear Creek. Had I gotten the job in Greenville, I would have had to drive 30 miles at night to work, but at Clear Creek, I could walk to work each day. God knows what is best for us.

God had brought this country boy a long way as he received his Bachelor of Science Education degree that May morning at Cumberland College in 1965. The dropout who left school because he was doing so poorly in 1952 had finished three years of Bible studies and received a college degree in 1965. Many skeptics would say that I had just found myself and was able to accomplish these years of work. But I know better. God had taken ahold of my life and was working out His plan for me. This is not a fatalistic approach that I had taken. I am aware that it took hard work on my part and my family even to get to this point in my life. It is my belief that God provided all the ability, strength and means for this to be accomplished.

Chapter 26
Staying at Concord

When I finished Cumberland College, I had been pastor of Concord for almost four and a half years. These had been good years. Pastoring and attending college was very tough on my family and me, but I enjoyed being busy. I really felt that the church and I had been blessed. The church was not able to pay a large salary, but we were able to survive. Some of the members of Concord probably felt that I would be leaving the church after I had finished college. In fact, I did preach a trial sermon at another church, but it was not the Lord's will for me to leave.

It is just marvelous how God works things out for His children. In order to stay at Concord, I would need a second job. When the new school year began, one of the teachers from our church had to be absent due to sickness. He asked me to substitute for him. The school was about one mile from the church. This was a challenge for me because he was teaching the fifth grade. As the weeks passed on, my teacher member did not get any better. It became obvious to me that he would have to resign. I had begun to love teaching and felt that this was God's way of letting me stay at Concord. It is not my intention to give any idea that God caused the other teacher to get sick for me to get a job. When it became official that the teaching position at Flat Lick was open, I decided to have a talk with the superintendent of schools about the job. He was very courteous and stated that he would like to see me have the job, but my certificate would not allow me to be classified as a fifth-grade teacher. I was certified to teach eighth grade through twelfth grade. He could have gotten me an emergency certificate had he not had teachers who were qualified to teach the fifth grade. He had several teachers who were qualified and wanted the job. I had already been offered another job with the government. When I got back to school, I informed the principal and my teacher friends that I would be leaving in a few days. After I explained to them about the certification problem, several them seemed to be rather upset. According to them, they knew of other teachers who were teaching out of their field of certification. The superintendent had his job to do, and I found no fault with that. As I left my schoolroom that afternoon, I fully expected it to be my last week at school.

The next morning, I was quite surprised when the principal came up to me and said, "The job is yours if you want it." Those words came as a very pleasant surprise to me. According to the principal, many of the parents and teachers had gotten in touch with the local school board member and the superintendent requesting that I be kept at the school. Instead of staying with the fifth grade, I was given the eighth grade. My duties included teaching English, science, health and reading to the eighth grade and English and health to the seventh grade. I was thankful for the confidence that the teachers and parents had placed in me.

Chapter 27
Growing with the Students

It would be foolish of me to say that things always went according to plans at the school. Anytime you have students whose ages range from 13-16, you are going to have moments of anxiety. It is amazing what you can overhear students saying about you. One student said during a class discussion, "I sure would like to poke him in the nose." If you do not know what "poke" means, it simply meant that he would have loved to flatten my nose with his fist. Some of the girls made fun by saying that I was "tall, dark and handsome." Naturally, I knew that it was true!

My greatest thrill as a teacher was to see students learn. My methods of teaching were not too difficult, but they were demanding. I did not expect a C student to do A work, but I was disappointed if he did not do his best. My English students did not appreciate it when I required oral reports. They knew that I would grade them on how well they performed in the areas of speech, grammar and overall presentation. Some students who could barely read gained self-confidence when they realized that I really wanted to help them. I promised my class that I would not fail any student who honestly tried to learn, but that I would fail a student who could do A work if he did not try. At the end of the year, I did have to fail some students who just did not try. Word got back to me that I would be overruled, but when I checked with the superintendent's office, I was informed that it was my decision to make. I made the decision and was not overruled.

When I taught school, the teacher was allowed to be in control of his students. My students made me an oak paddle and called it "old Betsy." You can be assured that I used it. Certainly, I did not abuse any students, but they knew who was in charge.

Schools have designated areas to smoke. This was not true in my area from 1965-68. Students would smoke, but they would sneak around and do it. One student did this with me one day, and he almost swallowed his cigarette when I walked in on him.

Flat Lick was an elementary school with grades 1-8. The athletic program consisted of basketball and football for the boys. One coach was in charge of both sports. What a surprise, when I was informed that I had to coach one or the other. I did not know anything about football and even less about basketball. I had played a little run and tackle football, but I did now know anything about coaching. When it came to basketball, I could barely get it through the hoop. If I was going to remain as a teacher at Flat Lick, I had to do my part with coaching. I chose football. Most of the players were back from the last year's team, and they could help me with the plays. Can you imagine a coach having to be taught by the players? The team members had the plays diagrammed from last year. Our first practice game was with the team that had won the district championship the year before. We played them on their field, which looked much like a cow pasture. That team pushed my boys all over that field that evening, and the game ended zero to zero. We were lucky, and I was angry because of the way my boys played. When I got back to the school, my quarterback got out of the car with a Coke in his hand and a grin on his face. When I got through with him, his grin was gone, and he was ready to get rid of his Coke, I said to him, "If you are going to play ball for me, I am going to practice each of you until you learn to play. If you do not agree with me, you had better quit now." He did not quit, nor did any of the other boys. I put on some practice clothes and made them block and tackle me. It is not easy for a seventh or eight grader to move someone weighing 210 pounds, but they tried. They learned the plays we had at the beginning of the season, plus some new things we tried. When the season began, the boys were ready. By half time, in most of our games, we would be further enough ahead that I would have the boys hold the score down. During one game, we were leading by 30 points, and the quarterback called time and asked what to do on fourth and four. I told him to punt the ball, and he immediately went back to the huddle and went for the score. He made it, and I did not say anything until the game was over. When all the boys got on the bus after the game, I requested that all eleven players who were on the field when I had ordered the punt to meet me in front of the school the next morning. My halfback, almost crying said, "Mr. Benenhaley, if you are going to paddle us, I am going to quit." I assured him that I was not going to paddle anyone. The quarterback tried to take the blame for disobeying me, but I knew that they all should have known better. When I got to the school the next morning, all but one player was waiting. I made them run three laps around the field before class. The other student came to class late, and I had him run the laps before he could come to class. You would not like me as a coach, would you? The next time those boys were in doubt about a play, they consulted with me before they did anything. Discipline was strict, but I do not recall one player stopping because of it.

When the season was over, the championship game was held between our school and the champions of the past year. This was the same team that we had played to a draw or tie at the beginning of the season. My boys were afraid the first time they met the champions, but this time they had gained experience and confidence. The opponents appeared confident that they would win. When the game began, their confidence soon changed to concern. My boys did not let them gain an inch on the first play of the game. The sound of the blocking and hitting could be heard from the sidelines. I knew that my boys were doing their jobs when I heard a member of the opposite team say, "Come on, we are not afraid of them." At the half, the score was tied six to six. The co-captain came over to the sidelines, almost crying, and said to his teammates, "Fellows, we must win this game because if we don't, you know what is going to happen." He was afraid that I would make them run laps again. The second half was a defensive battle. We came close to scoring several times, but the other team held. With time running out, and the ball on the opponent's ten-yard line, my quarterback called time and came to the sidelines to ask what should be done. I told

75

him to run an end sweep to either side of the line with his halfback carrying the ball. He did, and to the delight of the Flat Lick fans, he scored. The extra point was missed, and we led 12-6. The game was ours if we could hold them for the next minute. On the kickoff, the receiving team tried a reverse to fool our team, and for a breathtaking moment, they did just that. As the ball carrier streaked down the field, my son, Clayton, finally figured out who had the ball and hit the runner slowing him down enough until another teammate brought the ballcarrier down. During the season, I had not used Clayton much because I was afraid that the other members of the team might feel that I was being partial to my son. The assistant coach and players finally came and told me that I was not being fair to Clayton. Clayton proved that night that he could play. My boys held, and we were conference champions. After the game, I tried to shake hands with the opposing coach, but he refused and accused my team of playing dirty. This certainly was childish because my team had played a super game. The season had been one where the boys learned to play together and have a good time. After the game, the team presented me with a plaque that read, "In appreciation of our Coach, E. Benenhaley, from the Football Team Flat Lick, Kentucky 1967." The plaque meant a lot to me, and I have it in my office where I show it with pride.

Some important decisions had to be made when I took the coaching job at Flat Lick. My priorities had to be put into proper perspective. Since my first obligation was to the Concord Baptist Church, what would happen if the football games were scheduled for Wednesday nights during prayer meeting? When we, as coaches, met to schedule the games, I let them know that I would not play during church time. I was delighted that all the coaches agreed to schedule the games where they would not conflict with church services. It is tragic that so many school events are scheduled during Wednesday nights. Something is wrong with our Christian convictions. If coaches, teachers and administrators would demand that programs be scheduled other times rather than church nights, it could be done. If mothers and fathers who are Christians would stop supporting programs which are planned during church time, they would be changed to some other time.

My experience as a coach taught me the importance of letting players know that each one was important to the team. The coach who curses or always puts his players down might win some games, but he will never build the character of the players. I learned the importance of self-discipline, myself. It did not take me long to realize that I was trying to do too many things. It was tough to teach five and a half hours, practice football two hours, come home and visit church members and grade papers at night. My doctor really gave me a chewing out when I went to him with stomach problems. He asked, "Why come to me? You know what the problem is." I also learned that every church should try to pay their pastor enough in order that he might devote full time to that church. Some of the motivation that I tried to instill in my students in the classroom flowed over to the ballfield.

A highlight of every Flat Lick eighth grade class was the annual trip to the capitol at Frankfort at the end of the school year. The students would make money for the trip by selling candy. They usually made enough money to charter a Greyhound bus for the trip. Naturally, on my first trip with them, I was not sure what would happen. I had boys and girls who could make things rather exciting. I must say that each group that I took behaved very well. In fact, the guides at the capitol told me that my group had some of the best-behaved students that had been through the capitol. As we made preparations for one trip, word got to me that some students had removed some items from a gift shop the year before. I told my students that if I caught anyone taking any items that I would personally take them back to the store where the items were stolen. They knew that I meant what I said. I asked all the students to look their best for our last trip together. Long hair was just beginning to be popular in 1968, and I asked some of my boys to get a haircut before they came the next day. Some of the girls called my wife to find out if it would be alright to wear pants the next day. My wife assured them that this was a decision that they should make. The next day, the girls were well dressed, and the boys had haircuts. We had a delightful time, even though Timothy, our baby boy, became sick after eating a sandwich that some of the girls had prepared for me. I think he learned to turn down, after that, anything the students prepared for me.

    It is amazing how God works things out that seem impossible. When I started teaching, I realized that I was taking on another full-time job. Yet this was an opportunity for me to stay with the church and better provide for my family. It also meant that I would have opportunities to witness to boys and girls. Some of those students never attended church anywhere. I had some very unusual situations happen while I was teaching. Some of the people who had moved to Detroit and Ohio from the Flat Lick area would call the funeral director and let him know that they wanted to have a funeral conducted at a certain time. They would do this without consulting me. The director would get in touch with me and find out if I could conduct the funeral. As I stated in the beginning, Flat Lick School was not far from the church. When it became necessary for me to be away from the school, the principal was very understanding and would take charge of my class. It even worked out that I was able to leave one week and conduct a revival service at my home church of Long Branch.

Chapter 28
Preparation for Seminary

The idea of a seminary education would not leave my mind after I graduated from college. I felt that teaching at Flat Lick was making it possible for me to get some financial problems taken care of in order to get a seminary education if the opportunity came. While I was at Cumberland College, I discussed the possibility of attending New Orleans Seminary with an official of that school. He informed me that I possibly could get secular work in order to provide for my family and later get church work. Since I had been in the pastorate for several years, I did not like the idea of not being able to pastor. The representative suggested that my wife get a job also. I did not like that idea at all because my wife had not taken a public job since we had been married. Many wives work, and that is fine, but I wanted my wife to be home with the children. Having hot meals and a comfortable place to come to each day probably had me spoiled also.

All the Southern Baptist Seminaries provided an excellent education, but I had been told that Southeastern provided a better opportunity for church work. When I contacted the director of field education at Southeastern, he assured me that he would help me try and find church work. My wife and I drove up to Southeastern one day and looked the area over. Later the director called and asked if I would be willing to preach at a church near the Virginia line. Nina and I spent the night at the seminary and traveled to the church the next morning. This church had been having student pastors in the past. All the people were very nice, and the services went very well. After the morning service, I met with the pulpit committee, and they told me that they doubted if I would come for what they paid a preacher. They gave him $60 per week and provided a home. My salary teaching and pastoring was about $200 per week, I told them that I would come for $70 per week if we both felt that the Lord was leading. Later the chairman of the pulpit committee called and told me that most of the people voted to call me, but it was not unanimous. I do not know if the money was a problem or whether some just did not feel that it was God's will for us to come.

Since the door did not open for me to attend the seminary, I decided to continue my teaching for another year. The summer months, I thought, would give me an opportunity to rest some.

When the school year 1966-67 came to an end, a few cases of mumps had been going around. Two of my boys came down with them during Vacation Bible School. I did not have to worry because I had been in and out with all my cousins as a child, when they had those things, and was not bothered. Boy was I in for a surprise.

Everyone loves good news from home, but it is the bad news that causes the trips home to be long. One morning the phone rang, and my wife was informed that her brother's wife had died in her sleep. In order to leave for home, I had to go to Clear Creek and get a supply preacher for the Sunday services. It was rainy and the roads were very slick. As I traveled back from school, I suddenly realized that the truck in front of me was not turning off like I thought it was. When I applied the brakes, the car moved as if the brakes had not been applied. I could not go around the truck because another car was coming; neither could I swerve to the right because two spots for gas tanks were on the side of me. With a loud bang, I slammed into the back of the truck. From what could be seen, very little damage was done to the truck. The passengers in the truck stated they were alright. My beautiful little Ford was a mess. The front end was heavily damaged. It was obviously my fault. The highway patrolman was late getting there because his car would not start. A local deputy wrote up the account of the accident. I was not given a ticket, and I never knew why. The patrolman gave me a ride back to town. The local Dodge dealer loaned me a car to drive to South Carolina while he worked on mine. I did not get scared about the accident until I tried to fall asleep that night. When I would close my eyes, it seemed as if I could feel my car hitting the truck. We spent a few days home and returned to Kentucky.

My wife's niece came back home with us after the funeral. She got sick with some type of virus, and I noticed that some swelling had occurred under my ears. It could not be, but my wife informed me that I had the mumps. Well, I thought, if this is all it is, I am fine. I continued to drive the car and even walked up the church stairs. Now, I should not have done that. Mother came to visit us that week, and I was too sick to enjoy her. When I am too sick to eat steak and potato salad, I need a doctor. I had to go to the local hospital to get some medicine. One of the nurses who knew me laughed when she saw my swollen neck. She actually thought it was funny, but if I had not been so weak, I would have loved to spank her. The pills the doctor gave me cost $.50 apiece. I do not know what kind of pills they were, but I saw a casket pass in front of the mirror after I took one. It did not take me long to get rid of those things. I could endure the pain better than looking at a casket.

After I got better from the mumps, my family and I intended to take a vacation. We had to wait until my car had been repaired. The Ford was heavily damaged in the wreck, and it took some time to get all the parts. The day before we were to leave for South Carolina, I had been told that my car would be ready. That next morning the car was not ready. By this time, I was really angry. I was so angry that I decided to see what kind of trade the Dodge dealer would give. The owner tried to sell me a Dodge 500 Coronet, but I did not like the body style. About that time, the owner drove up in a firetruck red car. It was sharp, and I immediately asked the price. The owner informed me that he really did not know that I would want a red car being a preacher. My wife let him know that she liked red, and it was no one else's business about the color because we would be paying for it. After some figuring, he told me what he would take in addition to my car. After I made him a counter offer, we agreed to terms. We packed our things in that new car and started for South Carolina. It was quite a change from the old 1946 Ford we had when we moved to Kentucky.

My last year of teaching was a good one. The students responded well, and I really felt a sense of being helpful to others. There were some students whom I failed to reach. This really did not make me feel that I had failed because I tried hard to help all my students. There were times when some parents thought that I had been too demanding with their children. One mother threatened to take out a warrant for me if I did not apologize for taking a paddle to her son. He was about sixteen and thought he could run over the smaller students. I did not apologize, nor did she take out a warrant. In fact, she apologized to me later.

Chapter 29
Entering Seminary

Making a decision to drive 369 miles one way to school was not easy, but that is exactly what I did in June of 1968. The roads from Flat Lick, Kentucky to Wake Forest, North Carolina were long and lonely. But I had to know what seminary was like. If it was God's will for me to attend seminary, I had to start sometime. I felt that a summer session would provide some answers for me. The director of the field office at the seminary had promised to help me find church work if possible. When I arrived at Southeastern on that Monday afternoon, a note was on my door asking that I report to the field office. When I arrived at the office, a worker asked if I could meet with a pulpit committee on Tuesday night. Naturally I agreed to meet with the committee. When the committees came to the seminary, they usually interviewed several students and then requested that the one they chose be sent for a trial sermon.

I met with two committees. One did not seem very enthused with me, but the committee from Windsor, North Carolina seemed very interested. They were from the Siloam Baptist Church and had been using student pastors for some years. They gave me some information about the possibilities of their church and what they would be able to pay. After I listened to them very carefully, I explained a little bit about my background and preparation for the ministry. I informed them that I was of Turkish descent and that my family was dark-complexioned, like me. They knew that I was of the white race just like them, but I asked them to inform the church of my Turkish background. In fact, I told them that if any of their members did not like me because of my background, I would not want anything to do with their church. The members of the committee laughed and assured me that they could not see any problem because of my name or dark complexion. My reaction here might seem childish to some, but it is a very sore spot with me because of past attitudes that I have experienced. Because of my name and dark complexion, I have been asked if I were an Indian, Jewish, Spanish or whatever. There is one advantage that I have over those who are fair-complexioned. I do not have to buy any suntan lotion. Most men like to think of themselves as being tall, dark and handsome; at least I can say that I am tall and dark. The committee left Southeastern that night, and I did not know whether I would ever hear from them again.

After I talked with the pulpit committee, I started classes the next day. What a surprise when I entered my church administration class. Since I had been pastoring for several years, I felt that I had a good grasp of church work and the doctrines of the church. Seminary was very different from Bible School. In Bible School, we studied issues from a practical stance. Having come from such a background, I was not prepared for the theoretical approaches that I suddenly found myself facing. Knowing what Baptists believed about the Lord's Supper, I chose this subject for a class project. Afterall, is it not true that Baptists believe that the Lord's Supper is a "symbol?" When I made that statement in class, I thought some of the students would eat me alive. This type of attitude caught me by complete surprise. We argued in Bible School, but it was over different methods of Biblical interpretation. Nervously, I tried to answer the students' questions with scripture. Strange as it may seem, they were not concerned about what the scripture had to say. They wanted to know what I meant by "just a symbol." They had caught me in the trap of saying something without thinking it through. At first, I thought the students were just a bunch of liberals who did not believe the Bible. Certainly, I was not saying that the Lord's Supper did not have any meaning. It was, and still is, my belief that the Lord's Supper does not have any saving power in the act; but rather that it brings to our memory all that our Lord did for us in the act of redemption. Although there is not saving grace in the bread or wine, the very act of participation should cause every Christian to examine himself and ask for cleansing and renewing in his life. What a blessing and relief when some of the older students came to my rescue in class. They informed the questioning students that I was very much right in the use of scripture that related to the supper. My main problem was using language that seemed to give erroneous meaning to the supper. From that time forward, you can be sure that I was careful about the terminology used. To be quite candid, I kept my mouth shut most of the time. There were times when I would have to speak up about certain issues.

After the first week in school, I returned to Kentucky and to my family feeling that something special was about to happen. I did not mention anything to any of the members about having talked to the committee from Siloam. Every outward sign pointed to the fact that my work at Concord was coming to an end. Many of the young people who had been a vital factor in the success of the early years of my ministry had either married and moved away or were away in college. As a result of this, all phases of the church work were down. The next Monday morning I left for the seminary and arrived that evening. In the meantime, the pulpit committee from Siloam had called and requested that I come on Wednesday night for a trial sermon. This probably sounds strange to some, but I had told the committee that I could not be away from Concord on a Sunday.

A student friend of mine rode with me as far as Williamston, North Carolina on Wednesday as I traveled to Siloam. His father had pastored in Williamston, and he went to see some friends. Before I went to the church, I stopped by the home of one of the pulpit committee members and met his family. This was a delightful family. On the way to the church, they took me to see the parsonage. It was a fine brick home, and I knew that Nina would be pleased with it.

Usually just a few people attend most prayer services, but for a country church, the crowd at Siloam was impressive. My message was well-received by the congregation, and I felt a very friendly welcome to the community. It really appeared that God was making a way for me to attend seminary and minister to the people at Siloam Baptist Church. One lady gave me some ham sandwiches to take back with me. When I picked up my student friend and told him about the sandwiches, there were none left when we got back to the school.

As I returned home on Friday, there was an atmosphere of expectancy. The chairman of the pulpit committee had told me that he would phone me on Sunday night and let me know if the church had issued a call. I knew that the Lord had been directing me toward the seminary. Now that doors were beginning to open, frustration set it. Seven and a half year are a long time to stay with a church. Many things had happened during that time. Not only had Concord made it possible for me to attend college, but I gained valuable experience as we worked together. I had recognized that under the leadership of God, I had become somebody. The people in the community had accepted me as a leader in their church and community. The Concord Baptist Association had chosen me as the moderator, and I had been elected from the association as a member of the General Board of the Kentucky Baptist Convention. Parents and students looked to me for guidance in their school. This made me feel important. The feeling of importance was not one of arrogance, but one of thanksgiving. The mountainous people of Kentucky reminded me of my own people in South Carolina. They were close, clannish and had a particular culture all their own.

Chapter 30
Leaving Concord

The Sunday after my trip to Windsor found attendance way down at Concord. This was not a new happening, but it really bothered me that morning. The handwriting was on the wall. My effectiveness at Concord was over. It was not that my preaching had gotten worse or that the people did not love me; an atmosphere of change had come over the community. The government, thinking that policies provided were good for the people, had helped draw people away from church. Programs were provided for the youth while church services were going on. These programs were not designed to interfere with the church services, but they did at times.

Finally, I did what I knew was right to do. Without even talking with my wife, I went into the parsonage that Sunday morning and wrote out my resignation. You can imagine the surprise of my wife and boys as I read the resignation during the church service. After the service, one of the deacons asked me if I had any place to go. My answer was, "no", because I did not know if Siloam was going to call me or not. Following the night service, some of the members of Concord went home with us and asked that I reconsider my decision to resign. I thanked them for their love and concern and assured them that I had done what I felt was the Lord's will. While the members were leaving out of my yard, I received a call from the chairman of the pulpit committee at Siloam telling me that the church had issued me a call to become their pastor.

Ten of the most fruitful years of my life were coming to an end. From August 1958 until July 1968, God took care of my family and me in a very special way. Oh, I am aware that He always takes care of us, but these were very special years. These were years of trusting completely in the Lord. "Trust in the Lord with all thine heart, and lean not unto thine own understanding. In all thy ways acknowledge Him, and He shall direct thy paths" (Proverbs 3:5-6 KJV). I can tell the world that it is true that God takes care of His own. Praise His blessed name! So many times, God just reached down and showed us that He was near. He let us experience so many things that had to be His doings. The mission experiences near Harlan taught us so many things. I never shall forget the time Clayton fell out of the chair when the dear saint of God began to shout.

There were times of laughter. I am reminded of the Sunday afternoon when a goat came to our services. I had been called to preach the afternoon services at this little church near Pineville. Because of the heat, the church door had been left open, and the goat just walked in.

While at Clear Creek, I had the opportunity to preach at a little church near Harlan, Kentucky. After church, we went to have lunch with a family from the church. Wilbur, who was very young, asked to say the blessing. Being a gracious hostess, the lady of the house agreed for him to have the blessing. Wilbur bowed his head and said, "Amen, Brother Ben shot a rooster and killed a hen." You can imagine the laughter around that table. My wife and I would have crawled into a hole had we found one.

Money was very short in supply at Clear Creek, but Nina seemed to be able to make things last. She did not mind cleaning chickens for the school in order to get the necks and backs for our use. Nina did not attend school as long as I did, but she made good use of the things she learned at Clear Creek.

While we were at Clear Creek and during our first years at Concord, we did not have any hospital insurance. We could not afford it. God took care of us by using the good doctors at Middlesboro and Pineville. Not long after I arrived in Kentucky, I discovered that I had a lump in my left breast. According to the doctor, it was not anything to get alarmed about. When the lump failed to respond to treatment, the doctor decided that the lump must be removed. The doctor made no charge for his services. When any member of the family went to our doctor in Pineville, he made no charges. Clayton had his appendix removed, and the doctor did not charge a dime. When Timothy was born, the doctor did not make any charges for delivery, and the hospital gave a discount. Do not tell me that God does not take care of His children when there is a need. I believe with all my heart that God was directing the events in our lives. When I started teaching, I went to my doctor and told him that I wanted, and was able, to pay my bills. He said, "Let me worry about that." That is just what I did. If there was any worrying, he did it. There were times when our old car would have two flats at a time, but God would provide money for tires. God uses others to be a blessing to those who are in need.

When we moved to Flat Lick, some people visited our community from Ohio. Members of their church had heard about the needs of the people in the mountains, and they brought us a busload of clothes for me to give to the people in our community. The family who brought the clothes to us became very dear friends of ours. These were people we had never met before and yet the Lord sent them our way during a time of need. When Nina was having some medical problems, these friends from Ohio asked her to come see their doctor in Ohio. They offered us a place to stay plus they would get the appointment with the doctor. We accepted their offer and drove the 200 miles to see the doctor. The specialist corrected Nina's problem and charged $20. He gave Nina an appointment to see him again. The day for the appointment found the ground covered with snow. The roads were covered, and many who tried to travel them found themselves stuck or sliding off the road. I have not always done things that are normal, so we started to go to Ohio through all the snow. We made it by God's help. The doctor charged Nina $5 and said, "I am not going to charge you much after you have come this far in a storm to see me." He probably thought we should be seeing a "head doctor." That is the local term for psychiatrist.

When I entered Clear Creek, the thought of going to college never entered my mind because I was not sure that I would make it through Clear Creek. God knew best, and He opened the way for college. Since God had brought me much further than I had ever dreamed, some might not be surprised that the Lord opened the door for seminary training. It was, and still is, my desire to follow my Lord as He opens the doors of service.

The day finally arrived when we prepared to move from Concord. The committee from the Siloam Baptist Church had asked me to get a moving company from our area to move us, and they would take care of the bill. I got an independent trucker to move us because he was much cheaper. He and I loaded most of the furniture on a Thursday afternoon, and he left that Thursday night. My family and I stayed with some friends that night. What an empty feeling as we prepared to leave that Friday morning in July. We could not help but cry as members of the church waved as we drove away. There was not much we could say as a family when we drove through the community of Flat Lick and on through Pineville where we had spent so much time. We were leaving, but part of us stayed behind. The people of Bell County and Knox County had been good to us. We had met people who had been closer than any people other than our own families. I do not have any brothers or sisters, but many of those people stood by us just like they were family members. We were all members of the family of God.

When we arrived in Williamston, North Carolina, the entire family was ready for a hot meal and a good place to sleep. We stayed at a local motel that night. One of the deacons of Siloam and his family came by to see us that night, and this helped break the ice of loneliness for Nina and the boys.

Saturday was a busy day. The moving van arrived early that morning, and the task of getting things in place began. The church family helped tremendously, and this drew all of us even closer. Food was brought to the house for dinner and supper. It did not take us long to realize that these were our kind of people. When we went to bed that night, no one had to rock us to sleep.

Sunday morning came, and Nina was not able to attend church. She had a terrible sore throat. We had a very good morning service, and I could see that God was going to bless our efforts at Siloam.

Chapter 31
A New Church Field

The opportunities at Siloam would be limited because of the size of the community. The community surrounding Siloam was mostly made up of people who originally were farmers, but many of them now worked in the towns nearby. Very few of the people made their living solely by farming. The little town of Williamston was three miles from the church while Windsor was about five. There were church members living in both towns. My first move was to visit every member of the church and get acquainted with them. Next, we started a visitation program. The program of visitation was helpful although we did not have many people helping.

We lost one family just after I arrived as pastor. Brother J. N. Baggett was called as pastor of a church. I accused him of leaving because he could not stand sound doctrine. He and I still have a laugh about that.

Previous pastors of Siloam would stay at the seminary during the week from Tuesday through Friday. This kept the pastor from driving such long distances. The deacons would take care of the services while the pastor was away.

I certainly did not intend to break tradition, so I went to the seminary on Tuesday and came back on Friday. From the very beginning, I did not like this arrangement. My roommate was a pretty good fellow, but it seemed as if those walls would cave in on me. I had stayed in the dormitory during the summer, but I was too far from home to let it bother me.

My boys started school about the same month I did. It was Timothy's first year, and he did not like it at all. He conveniently developed a stomach ache each day, and his mother would have to get someone to get him from school. He continued this until I told his teacher not to call home again unless he was really sick. He finally got the message. All these problems for Nina at home made my stay at the seminary even worse. Not long after school started, Wilbur and Timothy had to be admitted to the hospital, suffering with colds that had almost turned into pneumonia. The doctor said that changing from one climate to another was the cause. Clayton really helped his mother during those days, and I am very grateful. I really feel that I took something away from Clayton during those days. He ran track at the school, and I never got to see a single meet. I saw him play one football game. He never argued, and really, it probably gave him a sense of worth as he helped his mother with the other boys.

Seminary was difficult for me. Reading claimed a large part of my time. Up to this point in my life, I had not been a serious reader, that is, reading to recall. Matters were further complicated when I had to read materials that I did not appreciate. I had to learn the hard way that different areas of reading were important if a person were to have a well-rounded education. I especially disliked reading any literature that used vulgar language. One student told me that I needed to read such books to know what was going on in the world. I reminded that young man that I did not need to attend seminary to find out that people used filthy language.

To listen to some people, you would think that all people who attend seminary are liberal or unbelievers. This is far from the truth. I met some very dedicated people at Southeastern. The following is an example: We had an archaeology class one day, and I felt that I was well-prepared. It was my responsibility to be able to name towns along the Mediterranean Sea during the ministry of Jesus. I had learned these towns in relationship to the sea and the desert. When I received my test paper, I froze. As I studied the map, I could not tell the land from the sea. Taking the paper and turning it in all directions, I still could not make heads or tails of it. My score was a 50% on the exam. I was crushed and went back to my room determined to quit school. Why not? I had become very good at quitting earlier I life. My teacher assured me that he understood and would help me make up the work. He was kind, but I wanted to make it on my own. If a college graduate could not make it in seminary, he had no business being there. When I got back to my room, I lay on my bed and began to feel sorry for myself. A young first-year student came by and had prayer with me. That does not sound like some unbeliever, does it? His coming by was just what I needed. From that day forward, I made good grades in archaeology. It was not easy, but I got by.

It was a thrill to leave Southeastern on Friday afternoons and start the one hundred miles to Windsor. It was a joy to be going home to Nina and the boys, and I knew that Nina would have a delicious meal waiting for me. God did not make any mistake when He brought Nina and me together. I doubt that I ever would have made it through school without her help and encouragement. She would have potato salad just about every Friday. I am a potato salad nut. I do not believe in divorce, but if I had married a woman who could not fix potato salad, that marriage would have been in trouble.

During hunting season, Clayton would want me to go deer hunting with him. I tried it a few Saturdays, but I would have to take a book on the stand with me. You can imagine the fun I had sitting on a deer stand reading about the ancient happenings in another part of the world. I never saw a deer. I do not know if one ever came close to me. Clayton was still glad that I went with him. He would have enjoyed it more had he been able to cut my shirt. If you missed a deer, the other hunters had the option of cutting the tail off your shirt. Usually they would cut the whole back out of it.

It was good to visit with church members during the weekend. Although my time was limited, I tried to visit as many people as possible. There was not much time for visiting because I would have to prepare two sermons for Sunday. The people were very kind and responsive at Siloam. In fact, they thought that I was a good preacher. They were so convincing that I began to think so, too.

After my first year at seminary, I was determined not to spend as much time away from my family the next year. During the summer months, I tried to make up for lost time on the church field. I had more time to visit and plan some church programs. Vacation Bible School was held during these summer months. Between those children who worked in the fields and those who played ball, we did not have many left. My boys played baseball, but they were not allowed to miss church services to do so. The team officials accepted them on the teams with that understanding.

Clayton worked in the tobacco fields during the summer, but I was not happy that he did. He worked hard and learned to provide for himself. He learned what hard work was when he chopped the grass out of peanuts. I was glad to see that he did not back away from hard work.

After the summer was over, I began my second year at Southeastern. This year was to be a much better year for me. I would be spending more time traveling, but I would be more content. I would be traveling four hundred miles per week rather than two. I would spend Tuesday night at the seminary and would return home Wednesday night for prayer service and return to school on Thursday morning. My new roommate for the coming year was Larry Holland. Larry was a true man of God and a true friend. He kept things lively for me. We argued all the time and some of the students actually thought we were angry with each other. Larry would not start studying until about 11:00 p.m. He was too busy running his mouth with the other students. After I would go to bed, he would come in and start typing. He would even have the nerve to call me and ask how to spell a word. Finally, I took all I could stand, and when he asked how to spell a word, I told him to look it up in the dictionary. He answered, "If I don't know how to spell it, how do you expect me to look it up?"

Larry loved to pull tricks on the students. There was one student who loved to say my name and then laugh about it. One day Larry took this student aside and said, "Boy, if you don't stop playing with Benenhaley's name, he is going to turn you every way but loose. Don't you know that it makes him angry for anyone to play with his name?" This young man took Larry at his word, and from then on, he handled my name very carefully.

During my spring break, Larry helped us in a revival at Siloam. This was a very good week for us. Larry stayed in our home, and the boys really enjoyed the fact that he would play ball with them. But during the preaching services, Larry was very serious and brought messages that both young and old could understand. Following the week of special services, I had fourteen for baptism. Many of these youth came from Nina's Sunday school class. We did not have a baptistry in our church, but the Edgewood Chapel Baptist Church let us use theirs.

In order to graduate in three years, I would have to attend a summer school session. I wanted to attend, but money was a factor. God knew my needs, and He had already made plans for me. Brother J. N. was building a new store and asked if I wanted to help him during the month of June. The working days were long and hot, but we had a good time of fellowship. J. N. was a very unusual fellow. I did not try to tell him how to build his store. He informed me that he had the plans in his head. When he marked a board and told me to cut it, I did, and I did not ask any questions. Any man smart enough to have the plans in his head must know how to mark a board. The strange thing about it all is that the boards would fit right in place. He still laughs when I say anything to him about the plans. I made enough money that month to attend the July term of summer school.

Criticizing others seems to be a trademark that many of us have. This certainly was true of me when I first entered Southeastern. I was very disappointed when I saw how few people attended chapel. To me, it was a disgrace for a ministerial student to miss chapel. By the time I was a senior, I was missing many chapel services because of the type of programs that were presented. Many of the programs sounded just like class lectures that dealt with theory rather than fact. When a good gospel message was brought, the service was well-attended.

As a first-year student, my name was mentioned for junior representative, but I was defeated. I ran again my senior year and won.

There is something about being a senior at any school that is special. There is more to it than just finishing. When you first enter a school, you are nervous, and many times, frightened. By that senior year, you know more people, you have finally gained your confidence, and you suddenly realize that you are somebody special. You do not necessarily mean this from an arrogant stance, but it is a good feeling to know that you have arrived at a very special place in your life.

As the final year came closer to the end, I could look back on my three years at Southeastern and see how God had taken care of my family and me. Here again was the man who, in 1958, did not know if he could make it in Bible school and receive a master's degree from seminary. Again, I say to the skeptic, God can take rough material and make it smooth. He can take an individual who has failed repeatedly and make him a success for Him. God was still moulding the clay for His service.

Several members of Siloam attended my graduation. Mother, her brother and his wife, and a dear friend attended from South Carolina. After the graduation, mother went home with us for a few days. Later we took her home and visited with her in South Carolina.

It was during my stay in the Long Branch community in June of 1971 that I really began to see the division that had occurred in the church. Thinking that I might be able to help the situation, I was asked to come later in August and conduct a revival. When I did help in a meeting, the Lord gave us souls for our labors, but the division was too deep to heal. This is not to say that the Lord could not heal the division, but it is to say that the Lord was not permitted to heal. During my stay that week, I was approached about becoming the pastor of the church. I informed the committee that I had commitments in North Carolina, which would run to the first of 1972. This was August of 1971.

Trying to determine what God's will was for me in North Carolina was not easy. The people at Siloam had been good to me. My family loved the area and the people. Clayton was in his junior year in high school and was really close to his friends. God knew all this, and it was up to us to follow His will. The summer of 1971 was a busy time for me because I had about six revivals during that time.

If I stayed in Windsor, I would have to get another job to supplement my income. A job at the Technical Institute in Williamston was offered to help in that area. I taught Biblical history at night and thoroughly enjoyed it. The students were eager to learn more about the Bible. During the early part of summer, a church committee from Kentucky called to see if I would be interested in coming to their church for a trial sermon. After some time of prayer and thought, I informed them that I was not interested in moving at that time. All during the fall and winter of 1971, the chairman of the deacons of Long Branch Baptist Church stayed in touch with me about coming to them as pastor.

It was an honor to be asked to return to my home church, or was it? The scriptures seem to say that it is not. "But Jesus said unto them, a prophet is not without honour, but in his country, and among his own kin, and in his own house" (Mark 6:4 KJV). This scripture puzzled and frightened me. In fact, I told Brother Wade Oxendine that the church better look elsewhere because I was not coming unless I knew, without a shadow of a doubt, that it was God's will. Some people in the Long Branch community may have felt that I would jump at the opportunity to come back home because of my mother. The fact is, my mother was not impressed about the idea of my coming back at all. Mother was afraid that I would not be accepted well because so many people were related to me. When I wrote Dr. R. G. Lee and Dr. W. A. Criswell and asked about the scripture in Mark, they both pointed out that it was not a matter of kin, which should determine whether I accept the church, but rather, it was a matter of whether it was God's will. By this time, I was having a tremendous struggle in really knowing what the Lord's will was. The members of Siloam did not know what agony I was going through. Shortness of breath and chest pains became a burden to me. Yes, it is true, preachers are human and have problems with nerves, too.

To me, it appeared that Long Branch was not going to look somewhere else for a pastor. How could I leave Siloam when the members had been so good to us? I knew, and they knew, that it was just a matter of time before I would make a move. The opportunities at Siloam were very limited. The church was best suited for a student pastor, but I did not want them to think that I used them just to get through school. The members knew that we loved them and wanted the best for them.

Instead of things getting better at Long Branch, they grew steadily worse. About half of the congregation withdrew to form an independent Baptist church. This split was inevitable before I was considered as pastor. The closeness of the people in the community made my decision even more difficult. I had grown up with many of those who pulled out of Long Branch, and many of them were close kin to me. How would they feel toward me for accepting Long Branch? Dr. Lee's answer to my letter took care of that question. It was not a matter of kin or how I felt about it. The crucial question was – is God in it? Brother Wade made an appointment to come and talk with me during November of 1971.

Boy, was it rough when Brother Wade arrived at our home on that November Saturday afternoon. We were having the torrential rains off a hurricane that was threatening to come inland. He and I went to the church after supper to discuss conditions at Long Branch and the possibility of my coming as pastor. Our discussion was very frank. The attendance was down at Long Branch, but with a full-time pastor, Brother Wade felt that this would increase. It is difficult to make demands without someone thinking that you are arrogant. If I were to return to Long Branch, it would not be as the little boy who went away in 1958. I would expect for my family and me to be treated just like any other pastor would be treated. If I could not have the respect of the members, there would be no need for me to return. I did not want to feel above or superior to anyone, but I did not want to be just one of the boys. I would not call people by their nicknames, and I would not expect someone to call me by a nickname. Brother Wade agreed with what I said and stated that he felt that things would work well. I agreed for the committee to present my name to the church with the understanding that I would not even consider the call unless it were unanimous.

Chapter 32
Leaving Siloam

No matter how hard I tried, the compulsion to accept the pastorate at Long Branch would not go away. Finally, I had to accept the fact that God was calling me to Long Branch. Later Brother Wade called and told me that the church had issued a unanimous call. My acceptance was not without fear and deep concern about my ability to lead the Long Branch Baptist Church. The next unhappy step was to resign from Siloam. This was difficult because we had grown so close to the members. To some degree, I felt that I was letting the people down. When I read my resignation and left the church building, it felt as though all my physical and spiritual strength had gone. My spirit was not helped when the members came crying and telling me how sorry they were that we were leaving. Being the gracious Christians that they were, they understood that I was following the will of the Lord.

According to some statistics, the average stay of a Southern Baptist pastor is less than two years. This is puzzling to me because I hate to move. I just wonder if God calls men away from churches that quickly. Nina and I packed some of our belongings, but we left most for the movers. Long Branch was sending a moving van from Sumter to take care of the moving. This made things easier for us because the company would be responsible for any things that were damaged.

Before we left Siloam that morning for South Carolina, we had lunch with our next-door neighbor. Nina had gotten very close to Louise as she had to all the ladies in the church. This is another reason why it was so hard for us to leave. When I was at the seminary, the ladies of the church would visit Nina and the boys and take Nina places to help pass the time of loneliness away. After we had lunch with our friends, we left for South Carolina. Nina and I drove the Volkswagen and the boys followed in the other car. This move was hard on the boys because they had made friends both in school and the community. Since the move was according to the will of God, we knew that things would work out fine. We arrived at the parsonage in South Carolina before the movers, and this made it possible for Nina to show them where she wanted everything.

Long Branch had agreed to build a den and storage room onto the parsonage before we moved. This would give us more room. About a year before we left Siloam, the church had added a beautiful kitchen and carport to the parsonage. Nina sure did hate to leave her beautiful kitchen with built-in stove and cabinets. Nina would not complain because she had always made what we had beautiful.

Chapter 33
Ministering at the Long Branch Baptist Church

The Long Branch Baptist Church is located in a rapidly changing community. When the church was established, it ministered to rural people. Today a rural church is facing an urban explosion. With the establishment of Shaw Air Force Base, Long Branch has been surrounded by homes. Figures received from the Sumter Census Department show that 7,536 people live in the Long Branch community.

The military brings to the community people from all over the world with different religious beliefs, cultures and educational backgrounds. Several military families have become a part of the Long Branch fellowship and have added to the strength and ministry of the church.

Long Branch can no longer use excuses for ministering just to "her own." The pastor, along with his members, needs to find the best way to minister to the needs of the community. It is understood that because of tradition, economic status and educational background, there will be some whom the church will not reach. These people will seek the church that best meets their needs.

If the lay people will be open to new areas of ministry, and if the pastor, with help from others, will train them, ministry will be enhanced.

God had called, and I answered that call to become pastor of the Long Branch Church. This pastorate would bring challenges that I had not faced at Concord or Siloam. At Concord, I learned to lead in teaching and building. My stay at Siloam was a time of challenge as we used what we had, in terms of resources, to reach others for Jesus Christ.

The month before I moved on the field at Long Branch, I faced a situation that was different than any I had faced at any of the other churches. Nina and I had been home for the Christmas holidays, and as we were leaving to return to North Carolina, we were informed that Nina's oldest brother had been killed by a shotgun blast. The family asked that I assist with the funeral. Since I had been called as the pastor of Long Branch, conducting the funeral of those who were close kin would have to be a part of that call.

My first responsibility as the pastor of Long Branch was to get the members organized to the point that they believed in themselves and their capabilities. Many of the members had always let "someone else" do the work. Since many the members had pulled out and started another church, the job could not be left to someone else. If the work was to be done, every person had to be willing to share the load. In the very beginning, we needed a song leader and piano player. God took care of this by sending us a young military family who blessed our hearts in this area. When this couple was called to another field, God sent others to take their place.

I found that the members accepted my family and me and tried very hard to help in the areas of need. As I stated in the beginning, I was afraid that there would be those who would not respect me as a pastor. This was a fear that was unfounded. In fact, most of the members were respectful. I had always had good deacons in other churches to work with, and Long Branch was no exception.

Some were disappointed when the church was not filled to capacity. Crowds did not come for Sunday school and other services as we wished, but God gave us the strength to move together. As in any church, there were victories and defeats. God even used the defeats to strengthen us.

Because the community was close-knit, I believe that God called me to Long Branch. I knew the people who had moved away from Long Branch as well as those who remained. As a result of this, I believe God used me in the community as a healing force. This was especially true when issues arose which could have been very divisive. I never tried to use my influence to get any person who had left Long Branch to return, but I did try to let all people know that I was near and would help if I could.

Long Branch made it possible for me to attend the Southern Baptist Convention in Philadelphia in June of 1972. It was my desire to keep the church informed about the work of Southern Baptists. That summer we sent a group of our boys to the Royal Ambassador Camp and our girls to Girls in Action camps. They enjoyed this very much, and I was glad to see the church concerned about the mission activities of our young people.

The next year I took my first airplane ride. The Southern Baptist Convention was meeting in Dallas, Texas. A plane had been chartered to take a load of preachers to the convention. I went, but I was scared. I sat between two preachers and hoped that we were close enough to the Lord for Him to keep that plane in the air. Once I got started, it was a good ride, but I was still scared. The trip to Dallas was very exciting. I traveled around with some fellow pastors from the Santee Association, of which, Long Branch is a member.

The convention met in Miami, Florida in 1975. In order for the church to be more informed about the workings of the convention, I asked the chairman of the deacons and his wife, Mr. and Mrs. Earnest Benenhaley, to attend with my wife and me. To save money we drove to Florida. We had a very good time together. After we got to Florida, and found our way around, we bought groceries and cooked our meals in our rooms. This sure did save us a lot of money, and it gave our wives the opportunity to help with the expenses. It is my belief that we should be careful how we use God's money. We could have eaten out, but it would have taken more time and cost more money. I have not attended a Southern Baptist Convention since 1975 because shortly after that meeting, I began to make plans to return to the seminary.

When I accepted the pastorate of the Long Branch Baptist Church, I did so with the understanding that I be able to return to school, if the opportunity arose. When I graduated in 1972, the Doctor of Ministry program was just getting started. This doctorate was geared to help the pastor perform more effectively in ministry in his own setting.

Chapter 34
A Time of Testing

Since God had already blessed beyond my early expectations with reference to education, you probably feel that I should have been satisfied with what God had done. To be truthful, the outlook for my being accepted in a doctoral program was not too bright. There would have been no problem of getting the degree from some of the home study schools. I am not knocking those kinds of schools because I am sure that they provide good training for many. But as for me, if I were going to spend money and time in school, I wanted a degree from an accredited school. One school wrote me a letter and offered me an honorary doctorate if I would give so much money to their library fund. It would have been much easier to have gone that route, but I needed the discipline of study.

    The Lutheran Seminary in Columbia would have been very close for me, but I was not able to present the type of topic for a research project that they required. The director was very kind and informed me that men have had to apply to a school several times before they were accepted. My scores on certain tests were not acceptable at Southeastern where I had done my Master of Divinity work. I was hurt because my own school had turned me down. I understood that they had rules to follow, but I felt that I had just been cut off without any concern about my feelings or desires. My frustration about not being accepted led to feelings about my school, which I hope were unfounded.

    Something kept the hope alive that I would still be able to work on the program leading to the Doctor of Ministry degree. I wrote for and received the catalogue from the Southern Baptist Theological

Seminary in Louisville, Kentucky. The program at Louisville was tough, but a student was given several tests to determine if he were qualified for the program. The faculty members who oversaw the Doctor of Ministry program at Southern gave much encouragement about the possibility of beginning and completing the course of study.

Even if I could make acceptable scores for entrance, there were still many problems. First, there was the problem of distance. Southern Seminary was about 600 miles away. It would be too exhausting to drive up on Sunday and return on Friday. Second, the cost of flying alone would be over $1,200. This would not include housing, food or books. Things still looked rather dark.

After some thought, I decided to travel to Louisville and just take the required test. The trip was long, but I stopped by some friends' home in Flat Lick, Kentucky, and spent the night. It was good to see these former church members again, and they encouraged me to stick with the schooling.

When I arrived at Southern Seminary, one of the first people to greet me was a former student friend from Southeastern. This was no accident. For the next two years, this friend was to meet me at the airport and bring me back every Friday afternoon. In addition, his wife was an excellent typist, and she did my typing while I was in school. Dr. and Mrs. Conyers are working in another state now, but God used them at Southern to help me get through.

After many discouraging weeks, I had given up the hope of being accepted at Southern. One Sunday afternoon, my phone rang and my friend at Louisville said, "Congratulations." When I asked for what, he informed me that I had been accepted to the Doctor of Ministry program. I was delighted, but where would the money be found?

Just as God had taken care of things in the past, he began to open doors again. Requests for me to assist in revival meetings began to come my way. All the churches gave much more than I deserved, but they wanted to have a part in my schooling. Members of Long Branch gave, and you could just see God moving in a marvelous way.

When I had my interview with an official from Southern, he wanted to know if I would come and spend the month at the school. The degree program was divided into J Terms. Some students would spend the entire month at the seminary to help with the expenses. I just told the official that I would not stay away from my family and church that long. Those men who stayed the months just had more fortitude than I did. I admire them because it must have been tough for them. I was homesick even before I left home.

My first J Term was in June. Boy was I afraid. The weeks were filled with work, but my newfound friends made things a lot easier. The work was geared to our needs. The areas of study were well planned and provided valuable insights into the meaning and practice of ministry. The books, which were required reading, provided help in understanding the pastor's role in a very complex society. I was able to make good grades, and this gave me confidence for the courses ahead.

The next area of study was to be one of the most strenuous of all courses. This was a one-week course which began on Monday and ended on Friday. Classes would be conducted during the day and night with homework each day. This course was called project methodology. Each student had to decide on a project that he felt would be helpful to him and the church he pastored. During that week, the student would learn how to gather materials, as well as refine his project. After we chose a topic, we would be divided into groups and discuss our topics and give advice and criticism about those topics. This type of study proved to be very helpful because we learned more about our own needs, as well as the needs of other students. At night, we would have to write reports about our project and turn them in the next day. It just so happened that the student who lived next door to me was an excellent typist, and he was kind enough to type my reports. God always provided for me in those areas of need.

The Doctor of Ministry program was so helpful because much of the work leading to the degree could be done on the church field.

In fact, particular needs or problems affecting the church could be used as areas of study. Another student and I met with a field advisor in Columbia certain times during the month to discuss problems that we faced. Our field advisor helped us in the areas of administration, sermon preparation and counseling. Our areas of study were not theoretical, but everyday problems that had to be dealt with in a loving manner.

The January J Term was the most difficult. It was difficult because of the cold weather and because of the nature of the studies. When I got off the plane in Louisville, during the month of January 1978, the ground was covered with snow. Instead of the snow melting, more came and made driving and walking very dangerous. Classes had to be cancelled because of the dangerous conditions. I was not sure that I could get to the airport on Friday and there was a good possibility that the airport would be closed. When I did manage to slide and slip to the airport, I found that my flight might not get in until later that night. Fortunately, I was able to leave on another flight. When that plane started traveling down the icy runway, I was afraid and thanked my Lord when we were finally airborne. The next week found the snowy conditions worse. As we touched down in Knoxville, Tennessee, the pilot had to gradually bring the plane to a halt to keep from skidding on the ice and snow. The same conditions faced us as we landed in Louisville. We could not have classes the next week, and since it was the last week of the course of study, our teachers talked about keeping us over the weekend. This did not set well with us at all. Although classes were not conducted, the students had been on campus. Some of the students who had chains on their tires even offered to go and bring the professors to the seminary campus. Our teachers met with us during a night session, and this kept us from staying over. When I arrived at the airport on Friday morning, my plane was ready to go, but the wings had to be de-iced before we could take off. This did not ease my fear any at all.

The last J Term in July of 1978 dealt with the human emotions. The professors gave us some tests, which gave us some ideas about the way we respond to those around us. The test pointed out some weaknesses in our personalities, but they also showed where and how we could improve.

Chapter 35
Seeking Ways to Broaden the Ministry of the Long Branch Baptist Church

The last phase of my studies leading to the Doctor of Ministry degree was to plan and write up the results of a project that dealt with some area of need at the Long Branch Baptist Church. Since there were so many needs, it would appear that such a project would be easy. It was far from being easy. The project had to be thoroughly researched, and the writing of the project had to be according to specific standards set forth by the seminary. The project had to deal with some current issue, and the goals of that project would be to find ways to deal with that issue in a helpful and informative manner.

My longing desire for Long Branch had been that the members realize their potential under the Lordship of Christ. With this in mind, I began to look for ways to challenge the members in that direction. No matter how much faith I had in the abilities of the members of Long Branch Baptist Church, those abilities would never be useful until each member caught the glimpse of his worth under God. My problem was getting them to see that worth. Too many members had been willing for the preacher to do all the work while others were willing for someone else to carry all the load. It is very convenient for church members to say, "I am not capable, or I would do it if I had the education." There are too many opportunities for furthering one's education for that to be an excuse for not working in the church. Many people do not want to take the time to return to school while others just do not have the proper motivation.

After much thought and study, I chose the topic, "Using Lay Renewal to Broaden the Ministry of the Long Branch Baptist Church," as my project. I liked the term, "Lay Renewal", because it dealt with the lay people in the church, and it spoke of coming alive. Dr. Earl Crumpler, who was at the time Director of Evangelism for South Carolina Baptist, provided an "Itinerary for the Journey" compiled by Reid Harding and David Haney. Both men were with the Home Mission Board of the Southern Baptist Convention. As I studied the suggested materials for a lay renewal weekend, I become more excited because I could see that this program was geared to the needs of Long Branch. The members, along with me, needed to get a better understanding of what it really meant to follow Christ sacrificially. The Brotherhood Department of the South Carolina Baptist Convention introduced a leader for the lay renewal weekend. This fine Christian leader brought together a group of Christian leaders from throughout South Carolina to lead us.

Before the lay renewal weekend began, it was my responsibility, along with a committee of leaders from the church, to study the ideas, background and needs of the Long Branch Baptist Church. The committee was made up of military members, members who grew up in the community, and young people. This committee met for several nights together and found that each person could be very candid with each other. The military members had an opportunity to tell how they felt about being a member of a church that had been called by some, "a family church." The military members stated that they felt very much at home and a part of the church. They did point out that they felt that the church should reach out to more people. Every member of the committee agreed that there was a need to reach out to the people around the church. Some members confessed that they did not know how to witness to others. They felt that there was a need for some type of study which could train them in the area of witnessing. When the committee meeting came to an end, there was agreement that we were failing, as a church, to minister to all around us. The big question that remained was what were we going to do about the needs of those around us?

The big weekend finally arrived. I met with the workers at the church, and immediately I could sense that these were people sent of the Lord. Before the services began, we had a delicious meal that had been prepared by the ladies of the church. The fellowship meal just set the tone for the services, which were to follow. As I hinted in the beginning, the lay program was "people-centered." The director divided the groups according to ages, and we went to our classes. These classes provided the opportunity for people to discuss what as on their hearts. I was thrilled as people, who had not been accustomed to speaking out, began to share desires and needs in their lives. I was beginning to see timid people speak up because they trusted those who were their leaders. The next morning, we met in different homes and had a time of sharing and prayer together. The host home provided refreshments. The youth and children had their programs at the church. For lunch, the adults met downtown for a time of fellowship. The significant thing about all these meetings was the fact that they had been planned by members of the church. People who had taken very little part in things in the past were now leading. This was encouraging to me because I knew the people had the abilities to do much more than they had been doing. The program leaders were teachers, bankers, small business people and a judge. That Saturday night, we had another time of sharing together, and the Lord just blessed and drew us together. Sunday morning found the directors teaching Sunday school classes, and the head director oversaw the morning service. We had a lunch together, and the team members left for their respective places of service. Before this team came to our church, many members were nervous about meeting them because of their varied backgrounds. When the team members left, there was a close bond of Christian love and devotion. That night, our members shared together what they felt the weekend had meant to our community. Many stated that it was the best program that had ever been had at Long Branch. My heart rejoiced as young people and adults asked that a training program be started to teach them how to share their faith with others. A youth program began a result of the weekend. We had not arrived yet, but a movement was begun to see that Long Branch be the ministering church that God intended.

Now that the lay renewal weekend was over, it was my responsibility to put the findings and the effects of that weekend on Long

Branch in writing. God provided marvelously for me in this matter. I had met two fine young ladies at Southern who had done my typing while I was on campus. They agreed to type my project for me. Since their office was in the same building, one agreed to type the first draft and the other the final. My major professor's office was right across from them, and they were able to correct the rough draft, and I would send the other draft to my field advisor in Columbia. When I had finished making the correcting, which both teachers suggested, I would send the final draft to the secretary, and she would finish it and get it back to me. Things do not just happen like that. God led me to those young secretaries. They did a marvelous job.

After the project was completed, I had to travel to Louisville to defend my project before three professors. My major professor, my field advisor and a professor, suggested by me, were in charge. I was so frightened when I went into the room for the exam that I left the print of my sweaty hands on the table. My major professor must have known how frightened I was because he said something funny to ease the tension as he came in. He will never know how much his remarks helped me that day. The committee members were very kind and helpful during the hour-long oral exam. After the exam was over, I had to leave the room in order for them to give me a grade. When they called me back in, they gave me a 9 out of 12 points, which as a B+. The struggle was over. By God's grace, I had finished the course. That June of 1979, I received the Doctor of Ministry degree. My family, along with a dear friend, drove up to see me graduate.

Chapter 36
Lessons Learned

It would be incorrect to say that I understand all of God's ways because of what has happened in my life. It is my understanding that God has a plan for His children, and as a result of that, God works that out that plan and purpose according to His divine will. The words, "predestination, election and justification", have caused much debate in our time, and yet, when all the arguments are in, God's way will still prevail. God is all-powerful and all-knowing. I just trust that I will always be willing to accept His will and purpose in my life.

The past 25 years have taught me some beautiful, and at times, painful lessons. My early years, because of the attitude of some people toward my family's ancestral background, prepared me for a life of inferiority. The type of school that was provided added to that feeling of inferiority. There were times on my job when I felt that I was given the hard or dirty job because of who I was. That may not be a fair judgment, and I trust that I was wrong. These feelings of inadequacy led to greater fears when God called me to preach. My fears were not relieved when one door after another was closed when I tried to enter school. Sure, I had the fear of not being accepted in school or in church. Why would people be different in other states? My resentment of the way some people had treated my own people had blinded me to the fact that there were good people in my own home county. All people in the area were not prejudicial, nor did they think of me as being inferior.

It is impossible to list all the ways that God touched our lives through others as He guided me through Bible school and college in Kentucky. God used all these blessings to make me aware that I was a special creation of His and had abilities that could be used for His service. From the very first day of Bible school until I left Kentucky, God provided. He gave me the strength to excel at Clear Creek. He provided money for college and a school teaching job after college. These happenings were acts of God.

Just at the right time, God opened the door to seminary and provided a wonderful church. He let me get to know wonderful people at Concord in Flat Lick, Kentucky and sent me to Siloam where a lovely group of people would provide for us during seminary days.

Does it seem strange that God would lead me away from Long Branch to prepare for the ministry and then lead me back? The way everything has happened would have to be according to the plan of God. When I came back to Long Branch, I was not only afraid of how I would be accepted in the church, but I was even afraid of how I would be accepted in the church. I was even afraid of how I would be accepted in Sumter County. God took care of all that. The people at Long Branch have been great. Most of the members are proud that I was their pastor, and they appreciate what God has done in and through my life. I have been well accepted by the Santee Association. Since I have been back in Sumter, I have served as president and secretary of the Santee Minister's Conference and served as moderator of the Santee Baptist Association.

God has worked wonders in my life and that of my family. There are still fears in my life. Since my children have become older, I fear for them in an age of sin and rebellion against God. My boys continually say that they have accepted Jesus Christ as Savior, but it is my longing that they let Him be the complete Lord of their lives. They have a tremendous advocate in their mother who holds them up to God in prayer. If I fail with my own children, I feel that I have failed in my first responsibility as a Christian. But by experience, I know that God can do those things that seem impossible to us. I am still praying for the day when my boys will give their abilities completely to the Lord for Him to use in His own way. Just as God has taken Nina and me and moulded us for His service, He can do so with our children. God has promised that children will remember Him, if they have been brought up according to His Word. Nina and I have not been perfect, but we have tried to bring up our children in the fear of the Lord.

Where God will lead from here, I am not sure. How much longer He will allow us to stay at Long Branch is not known. It is my desire to be in His will. When He gets ready for us to move, He will let us know. It is my desire that I always listen and follow His directions. God has not failed us in the past, and I hope that I will always remember that vessels moulded by the Master are to be used by Him.

Chapter 37
Leaving Long Branch

It is never an easy decision to leave a church where you are loved and respected. There were several factors that I had to face when the time came for me to move to another church. At Long Branch, I was close to my mother, and I could help in her older days. My boys had spent most of their teen years in this community, and I knew that they did not want to leave. Nina's brothers and sisters lived close by. All these factors were important, but I knew that these must not be the factors that would determine whether I would move or not. God had led me to Long Branch, and it must be God who would determine when I should move.

Deep down inside, I felt that God was ready for me to move. I had been at Long Branch nine years, and God had used us together. Some important foundations had been laid, and probably another leader could lead the church in a more effective ministry.

When a pastor friend asked if he could present my name to another church who was looking for a pastor, I agreed with the understanding that he must feel God's leadership in this matter. When I mentioned this to Nina, she did not seem impressed at all. When I saw Nina's reaction, I really began to wonder if God wanted my friend to present my name to the church. Nina had always stood with me in my ministry, and I knew that I could not be effective at another church unless my wife stood by me.

My friend had talked to me about the Sweetwater Baptist Church of North Augusta back in August of 1980. It was September when the chairman of the pulpit committee called and asked if his committee could come and talk with me. The chairman told me later that I did not sound very excited when I told him they could come.

It is a nervous time for me when I look out in a congregation and realize that a pulpit committee is there. When the committee from Sweetwater came to hear me at Long Branch, I was leading the singing, and this certainly did not help my nervous condition.

After the morning service, my wife and I had dinner with the committee from Sweetwater. It appeared that they were just about as nervous as my wife and I were. I had ordered a good-looking steak, but between answering and asking questions, it had gotten rather cold. I feel that the committee learned something about me, and I learned about their church community. We were rather frank and open with each other, and I feel this is as it should be. Many committees fail to find out all they should about some men before they invite them to their churches. Each should know the good and bad about each other. When Nina and I returned home, we did not have any clear picture of what God's will was for us concerning Sweetwater. By the actions of the committee, we could not tell how they felt about us. In fact, it would not have surprised me if we had never heard from them again. My pride may have been damaged, but I knew that it was possible that the committee was not impressed with us.

Nina and I tried to act naturally at the night service at Long Branch, but we could tell that many of the members wanted to know what was happening. We knew that most of the members loved us and did not want us to leave. That love was mutual because Nina and I loved the members very much, and it would be very difficult to leave, should Sweetwater call.

When I met with the deacons at Long Branch, I assured them that I had not been looking for a church. I let them know that no kind of agreement had been reached or discussed. In fact, I told them that I probably would never hear from Sweetwater again. One of the deacons replied, "Preacher, I look for you to hear from them again." I appreciated the attitude of every deacon at that meeting. Each stated that he would hate to see me leave, but he believed that

I would follow the leadership of the Lord. Their confidence in me will always be an inspiration as I seek God's guidance in my life.

On Wednesday, following the committee's visit on Sunday, I received a letter from the chairman of the pulpit committee from Sweetwater. It was a friendly letter stating that each member of the committee enjoyed the services and friendliness of the people at Long Branch. It further stated that they wanted to find out more about me and would get in touch later. This could have been a friendly way of saying, "thank you, but we will look in other places." I really did not know what to expect.

Some weeks later, the committee visited Long Branch again, and I had the opportunity to meet two members of the committee who had not visited before. At the dinner table, we had the opportunity to discuss some areas of concern at the church. I tried, as best as I could, to explain my position on a number of theological issues. They knew that I accepted, without reservation, the truthfulness and authority of the scriptures.

After this second visit by the committee from Sweetwater, the members of Long Branch were expecting me to leave. One dear member of Long Branch said to a deacon, "Tell those people to leave our pastor alone."

Early in November, Nina and I were invited to the Sweetwater Community to get a look at the church field and surrounding area. It was a cold, gloomy and sad day. The committee made us welcome to the church and community. A delicious meal was provided, but Nina and I were not impressed. Things just did not seem right for some reason. It just was not easy to find out what God's will might be for us. If the members of Long Branch had been trying to get rid of us, the decision probably would not have been as difficult. The people at Long Branch did not want us to leave and, deep down, we did not want to leave. Things were not moving like I would have liked to have seen them move at Long Branch, but I could have stayed without any problem. It is good to know that you are loved by a congregation and that you love them. Through all of this, God had prepared another field for us. As much as we loved the people at

Long Branch, little by little, God began to show me that He wanted me to move.

When Nina and I returned to Dalzell, after visiting the Sweetwater area, we had more doubts than before about our visit. It appeared that the pulpit committee was ready to ask me to come to the church for a "trial sermon." At first, they were concerned about my stand on divorce and remarriage. I had told them that it was my policy, based on what I felt the scriptures taught, that I would not perform any marriage ceremonies for anyone who was divorced. I tried to make it clear to them that I was not saying that a person could not be a Christian and be divorced, nor was I trying to be a judge. Each person would have to answer for his actions to the Lord and not to me. But I did say that I felt that it would be wrong for me to have part in any marriage when God's Word said, "no." I am well aware that there are many who disagree with my beliefs about this matter, but I am the only one who will have to stand before the Lord for me.

Since the church had some teachers who had been remarried, the committee felt that I might try to remove those teachers from their classes. I assured them that I would do no such thing. God is a forgiving God and forgives any sin, that is, if a person seeks His forgiveness.

Some weeks after our visit to Sweetwater, I received a letter from the committee asking me to come for a "trial sermon." This was in November, and since the holiday season was coming, they would be willing for me to wait until January to come. This made it much easier for us. I still was not sure about the Lord's will in the move, but I felt that I should preach for the committee since they had been so concerned about us. The date of January 15th was set.

When I let the deacons at Long Branch know about our decision to preach for the committee at Sweetwater, most of them were convinced that they were about to lose their pastor. They could sense and appreciate the struggle I was having trying to be sure of what God's will was in this matter.

The days leading up to January 15th were not easy, nor were they happy days. Many may have taken the days of unrest and indecision as a sign that God did not want me to leave Long Branch. My middle son had already informed us that he would not move with us. Wilbur was 23 years old, and what could we do? Tim, who was 18, would move with us, but did not want to leave the area. What were we to do? Surely if God wanted us to move, He would make things easy for us. But is this the way God works? Has He promised that things would be easy? Many would say that my first obligation is to my family. This thought haunted me as I tried to know God's will. Any man who cannot take charge of his own family will not be able to lead others, I reasoned. But through all the confusion, I could not get the Sweetwater Church out of my mind. Why would God permit my family to go through this time of testing? What was He trying to teach us? I never have been able to find the easy answers that some seem to find about the Lord's will.

Chapter 38
Meeting the People at Sweetwater

It was one week before Nina, Timothy and I would travel to North Augusta for a reception on Saturday night and the sermon on Sunday morning. The reception was given in order that we might meet the people and they, us.

On Monday, before we left on Saturday, Clayton, our oldest son dropped a bombshell at our feet. He and his wife were separating. We were crushed. We hurt for them and for ourselves. How could we face a church and tell them that our son and his wife were separated? These types of things do not happen in ministers' homes, do they? We are supposed to be perfect people! But suddenly, I realized that we were not perfect. Where had we gone wrong? Our children had been brought up in the church, we had family devotions and our children had made decisions for Christ at an early age. This must be a dream! It could not be happening to us! It was just as real as day and night. We could not close our eyes and wish the facts away.

I am afraid that I was thinking more about the embarrassment that my son's separation would bring to my ministry than I was of his hurt. Too many times, we think about ourselves and forget about the hurt of others. It would be an untruth if I said that I was not angry toward my son. Yet, I did not know then, nor do I know now, why their marriage did not work. It is my belief, based on my understanding of the scripture, that it is never God's will for a marriage to fall apart.

On the Saturday in January when we arrived at the Sweetwater Baptist Church, Dr. Charles Page, pastor of the First Baptist Church of North Augusta, met us and showed us around town. This was during the afternoon before we met the members of Sweetwater that night.

Our youngest son, Timothy, was not too happy about standing in a reception line that night. In fact, I was not too happy about the situation, myself.

As it turned out, the get-together at the church was a turning point in my decision to accept the pastorate of Sweetwater. The friendliness of the people really won us over. The people made us feel at home, and I realized that we could work together.

Sunday morning came, and I was rather nervous, but I could feel the presence of the Lord. I did not try to preach a "candy stick" message (one that really impresses the people and the best one a pastor has). My message related to the family, and I just could not help but cry when I explained that my son and his wife had separated just before we came on the weekend. Boy, I thought, I really blew it today. I felt as if I had really brought a very poor message. The subject was not poor, but I felt that I had done a poor job of delivering it. Whether the members were just trying to be kind, I am not sure, but many of them stated that they really appreciated the message. As to my weeping, they stated that they were glad to know that I was "human."

Two weeks after I preached at Sweetwater, the church issued a unanimous call for me to become their pastor. With full assurance that I was doing God's will, I accepted the call and resigned as pastor of Long Branch Baptist Church. This was not easy, but I felt that God would send a pastor to the Long Branch Church. When God calls a man away from a church, He has someone to take his place.

Chapter 39
Moving to Sweetwater

Moving is a nerve-racking job. Sometimes you feel like shutting your eyes and just taking many things and putting them in the trash. It is amazing how much people store over the years. Much of it could really be put in the trash. In fact, I burned a lot of trash.

At first, a moving van was to pick up our furniture, but some of the men at Sweetwater learned that they could borrow a rental truck. This would be much cheaper, but I was concerned about what would happen to our furniture. The moving company would have been responsible for any damage, but there would be no insurance if a rental van was used. I agreed for the rental van to be used, provided some insurance would be provided for my furniture. The men from Sweetwater were very careful with our furniture and did an excellent job of moving us. The men who came to move us were very friendly, and this helped my mother realize that I was moving among some great people.

The members of Sweetwater made our first days on the church field much easier by their helpfulness. They also made us feel a part of the community.

Chapter 40
The First Months at Sweetwater

It did not take me long to realize the great potential for growth and outreach in the Sweetwater community. One great need was to get the people to realize that potential.

Things did not move as fast as I thought they should. Attendance was not as great as it should have been. This caused some frustration for me, but I soon began to realize that this would take time. The summer slump really bothered me as many of our people would be away very often.

Nina and I were very concerned about the fact that Timothy was very unhappy. When he moved to the community, the job he expected to get was given to someone else. This really came as a blow to him. He got another job, but he was still unhappy. He finally got a job that he liked, but he still wanted to return to Sumter. Wilbur and Clayton were still in Sumter, and Timothy felt that he could make it there. He probably could have made it, but Nina and I felt that it was best for him to stay with us. There comes a time when one must be willing to let their children go and make a life for themselves, but we did not feel that it was time.

After about four months, Wilbur called and wanted to know if he could come and stay with us. I reminded him that Clayton had stayed in Sumter to help him, and he could not move in with us unless we let Clayton also. This was just what Clayton wanted. Pretty soon, we had all three of our sons with us.

You would think now that everything was fine, but it was not. Timothy was still unhappy, and Wilbur was ready to return every weekend to Sumter. Timothy really bothered us because he became so depressed. He would come in from work, eat his supper and just lay around on the bed or listen to "jungle music." That is what I call it. He just wanted to be by himself. He was miserable and made us miserable. Nina and I just continued to trust the Lord to take care of these matters.

After much work and prayer, things slowly began to move. The services of the church have an air of excitement, many workers are busy working for the Lord, new people are being added to the fellowship and we can see that God is still willing to bless. Clayton is happy at Sweetwater. Wilbur and Timothy still have Sumter on their minds, but they are trying to adjust. God will take care of these things.

My work as pastor of Sweetwater has been made easier because Long Branch has called a good pastor to lead them. I can feel that the people of Sweetwater love us, and this makes me want to be a much better pastor and leader.

Things have not been easy these past months. I am still hoping and praying that my boys will become more excited about what they can do in the service of their Lord. All three of our sons have much that can be given in the service of their Lord. God loves them, and He will continue to direct their lives.

Through all the frustrations of the past months, Nina and I are sure that God led us to the Sweetwater Baptist Church. It is our desire to be all that our blessed Lord wants us to be.

What we have, we owe it all to our blessed Lord. Any abilities that we might possess, we want them used for the glory of our Lord. For everyone who might read these pages, we want God's will and purpose to work through your life. For those who are not Christians, we want you to know the forgiveness that comes through Jesus Christ. God did not have the best to work with when He chose me, but thanks to Him, He was willing to mould rough clay for His glory. Pray for my family that we might become all that our Lord wants us to become.

Part Two

Introduction

Much has happened since the first part of Moulded Clay was written in 1982. These 36 years have been times of joy and sadness. Yet, through each year, God has been faithful.

In this next section of Moulded Clay, hopefully, the years at Sweetwater, Silver Crest and Red Hill, will be helpful to those who read about the victories and struggles along the way. Thank God for His grace and mercy as He has protected and cared for my family and me all these years.

Chapter 41
Applied Ministry
The Preacher

There is no greater calling in the world than to have the call of God to shepherd a church. God's call and instructions for a preacher are very clear (1 Timothy 3:1-7). No one should ever attempt to preach without, to the best of his ability, following the Bible's qualifications for a preacher. No church should attempt to change the Bible's rules or instructions for a preacher. To do so dishonors God and His Word! This may sound judgmental, but there are too many behind pulpits today who have never been called by God and are leading people astray (Jeremiah 23:1-2).

It has been my desire, and I have, by God's grace, tried to be faithful in preaching His Word (2 Timothy 4:1-2). A preacher cannot expect to be loved by everyone, if he is faithful, in preaching the Word (Luke 6:26). With all that God has given to us, He expects us to be faithful (Matthew 25:21).

When I became a Christian, the Bible was very precious to me. There was no doubt, in my mind that the Bible was true in all areas.

It was during my Bible school, college and seminary days that I learned such terms as, inerrancy (truth without any error), mechanical diction (God guiding man's Hand) and Dynamic Theory (inspired thought). For me, the inerrancy and infallibility of the Bible has been my guide.

God never called any preacher to preach theories about the Bible, but rather God's truth to the Church. Any person who tries to change God's truth for his opinions should not attempt to lead a church (2 Timothy 3:16, 2 Peter 1:20 and Matthew 24:35).

During my 21 years as pastor of Sweetwater, no person was allowed, if I knew it, to lead or teach, who did not believe in the authority and truthfulness of God's Word. When I became pastor, I wanted to know that I had the authority to be in charge of the pulpit. The church could be sure that any preacher who was asked to conduct a revival or Bible study would be a man who preached and lived according to the Bible.

The Pastor

Is every preacher of a church a pastor? He certainly should be!

Some might disagree, but a preacher must prove himself before he is accepted as pastor. How does he prove himself?

1. He must show his people that he is God's man. He does that by his daily walk with God and before his people (Romans 12:1-2). Church members must live holy and dedicated lives, but whether it is right or not, the preacher-pastor is expected to set a standard that is higher than that of the members.

2. The pastor must set some guidelines for his own protection. Recently, secular and religious papers have printed reports of immorality and sexual abuse by pastors and religious leaders. How tragic this is that such acts are happening in, among and between people who are supposed to be setting godly examples for others.

3. A pastor should always have someone with him when he is visiting. He should never visit in a home if there is no one but a female there. He should never counsel a woman by himself. The secretaries at Sweetwater knew not to leave the office if a woman came for counseling. If a female wanted counseling after office hours, she either would meet my wife and me at my office or at my home with my wife present.

4. A preacher and his staff should be very careful about hugging the opposite sex. There are times, such as a death, sudden tragedies, thank you or special events when a friendly or compassionate hug is appropriate

5. When should a preacher visit? There are those who think the preacher should visit their home just to socialize. Most preachers do not have time to just drop by. Certainly, the preacher should visit during times of trouble, sickness and death. When it comes to hospital visitation, things certainly have changed. Most preachers today will drop by a patient's room or surgery area long enough to say "hi" and pray and leave. If there were a serious surgery, and most surgeries are serious, I felt that it was my place to be with the family. The idea today is that preachers do not have the time to wait until the surgery is completed. As I remember, the minutes and hours are the same as always!

You see, a preacher becomes a pastor when he can be trusted, depended on, and called day or night. I am not talking about being called when someone has an ingrown toenail.

The Pastor at Work

Most people do not realize the joys as well as the heartaches of a pastor. The pastor is not a boss, but he is the overseer of the congregation (Acts 20:28). The pastor's job is to lead the church in worship by proclaiming the word of God with assurance and authority. He needs to let his people know that he believes and means what he says. He has been called by God to his position and not to seek his own glory. He is to lead his people by example and not for money (1Peter 5:1-3). He certainly is not to be a lazy person (1 Corinthians 4:1-2). A few examples when a pastor is needed are when there is a serious illness or death and when tragedy happens at the hospital.

Once, my wife and I were waiting with a woman while her husband was having a procedure, when suddenly the doctors began to rush by. The husband died on the table. The precious wife asked Nina to go with her to see her husband. I will never forget the doctor who went with me to tell the man's mother and children that he had died. At another hospital, as we sat in the waiting room, the emergency alarm went off and the doctor told the wife that her husband had died. While at the family kitchen table, the phone rang, and a voice said, "a terrible accident has happened on Sweetwater Road and you are needed". When I arrived, they were removing the dead body of a young man. The patrolmen wanted me to go and tell the grandmother. Two women EMTs went with me. I was so thankful that those ladies went with me. These are examples and just a few of the many opportunities that a pastor and his members must minister to hurting families. Fearing that I might miss some names, I cannot share the joys and heartaches that my wife and I have shared with so many. God has ways of showing people His power, mercy and grace during difficult times. One of our young boys in the church was struck by a car and was given a 25% chance to live. His parents, who were church members, trusted the Lord for his recovery. Today he is married and living a productive life.

As a Pastor-Preacher

As a pastor-preacher, I have had many opportunities to minister to my people. An excellent opportunity is to teach a new member class. This gives the pastor the joy of knowing the new members as well as the new members knowing him. This gives the pastor the chance to explain to the members the biblical doctrines and organizations of the church. It further gives the pastor the opportunities to explain the responsibilities and opportunities for service for the new member. It is also a special time for the members to ask questions. A new members class by the pastor can deter a lot of problems that might occur by members not knowing what the doctrines and responsibility of members are.

It causes more time and work for the busy pastor, but I enjoyed teaching the Master Life Program. This was one of the best studies for learning scripture and the doctrines of the Bible put out by the Baptist Training Union.

Marriage Seminars were another study that I found to be very helpful. With so many marriages in trouble, it was very helpful to bring in leaders and materials that could strengthen families.

The great opportunities afforded to me in the local churches and outside are in no way to praise me, but to show the providence, mercy and grace of Holy God. There are many who could share their life story of how God has worked in their lives. These next examples are to show how God used, for His glory, clay that needed to be moulded.

Revivals

1. In all the churches that I have pastored, but especially my 21 years at Sweetwater, I must thank these churches for giving me the opportunity to minister to others. From Washington state, Indiana, Ohio, Kentucky, Virginia, Tennessee, North Carolina, South Carolina and Georgia, the Lord allowed me to share the gospel with others.

2. Through service in the Southern Baptist Convention and State Convention, I wrote lessons for discipleship training for the Southern Baptist Convention, served on the general board of the South Carolina State Convention, served on committees for the Convention Program, served as Moderator of the Santee Baptist Association and Aiken Association, and served as vice moderator of the Edgefield Association.

In May of 1990, The American Association of Bible Colleges selected me to the Honor Society of Delta Epsilon Chi. I was a graduate of the Clear Creek Bible School, which is now a college.

Chapter 42
Organizational Ministries
Music Ministry

Music is an important part of the worship service. Godly music sets the tone for the preaching service. Years ago, we lost some members because I would not go to a contemporary music type, whatever type that is!

Some years ago, mainline churches were caught up in charismatic, tongue-speaking and very upbeat music. Today, many churches, including many Southern Baptist Churches, have gone to what they call contemporary music. Some churches have light-flashing music that is so loud that you need ear plugs and an interpreter to explain what is being played and sung. According to many, this type of music is to attract young people because this is what they want. The purpose of the church is not to give people what they want, but rather what they need.

Sweetwater has a blend of gospel choirs, quartets, solos and music that honors the Lord. Any time that churches use the world's methods to reach children, youth or adults they are playing Satan's game (1 John 2:15).

Any type of instrument, choir or specials, when used should be biblical, understandable and lead people to worship Holy God and not man. It is my prayer that Sweetwater Baptist Church will always provide music that honors God. Sweetwater has as many great musical abilities and voices as any church I have heard.

Sunday School

For some reason, Sunday School attendance is down in most churches. A number of churches have done away with Sunday School altogether. Why?

1. Some say that it is boring or does not challenge them.
2. Could it be that people are lazy or figure that the worship service is all that they need?
3. Could it be that we, as pastor and staff, do not encourage and support Sunday School? The pastor's class is a great time to encourage new members to attend and support Sunday School and the church programs.
4. The world has become more appealing to many than the church. Ballgames on Sunday have crippled many of our churches. It is not just the unsaved people but rather church leaders and members who have let the world and its programs take charge. If church leaders would stop coaching and umpiring, and parents would take their children to church on Sunday and Wednesday nights, our churches would be filled, and the athletic programs would have plenty of players, coaches and umpires during the week. All it will take is for enough parents to say "no" to the allure of anything that takes away our witness for our Lord and the support of His church.
5. A vibrant Sunday School strengthens the total church program. It is the Bible-teaching and soul-winning agency of the church. As a result, the preaching, attendance, evangelism, discipleship training and stewardship are encouraged.

You can see why godly teachers are necessary. Such teachers will live a godly life, lead in prayer and Bible study, plus be soul winners. In addition to having godly leaders and teachers, I sought to bring in great educational leaders from other areas who would train and encourage our own people.

For some reason, I do not know why, programs such as the Roman Road, The Four Spiritual Laws and especially the Faith Program are not used much today. This might be why more people are not being saved and baptized.

Sunday School is a great place to have fellowship and get to know each other. What an opportunity to reach the lost for Jesus, as well as to help your own members who might be in need. How many times have Sweetwater classes stepped in with giving when a family was in need? I testify to the many times that classes and individuals have brought meals or sent gifts or money in the time of need for my family. God will bless a Sunday School whose leaders and members have a desire to be their best for Jesus (Romans 12:1-2).

If I were to start a new church, it would be my desire to have the best Minister of Education possible. This person would have to be a dedicated director who, by example, would support the pastor, all the agencies of the church and be evangelical in the classrooms and the community. A church with such a director would be strengthened in all areas of ministry.

The Deacons

This group of men should have been mentioned after the pastor. The first deacons were chosen to assist the pastor (Acts 6:1-7). The Bible has clear qualifications for the deacons (1 Timothy 3:8-13). We are living in a day when many pastors and churches do not follow the plain teachings of the Word of God when it comes to ordaining deacons. No pastor or church has the right to change the qualifications of the Bible.

The word deacon means servant. He is not a boss or dictator. His job is to support the pastor. If the pastor goes contrary to what the Bible teaches, the deacons and church have the right to correct him.

The Family Ministry Plan is the responsibility of the deacon. Each deacon should have a number of families under his care. Too many times, I have heard members say, "I don't know who my deacon is". For any deacon, that should not be so! The deacon who truly does his job will minister to his family. This could be by a visit, a card or telephone call. When there is a physical or spiritual need, to the best of his ability, he should meet that need. By keeping up with the needs of his family, the deacon can help keep peace and harmony in the church.

I found it very important for me to teach new deacons what it really means, biblically, to be a deacon. In addition to the Bible, there are many good books and materials for help.

A godly qualified deacon should be able to speak in the place of the preacher, should the need arise. Stephen is a good example (Acts 7:55-56).

Youth Ministry

When I came to Sweetwater in 1981, the pastor and music minister were the staff aided by one secretary. As the attendance grew, the need for a person to lead the youth arose. When the search committee presented to the church a person for the youth minister position, a member of the church arose and said, "We don't need another staff member, we have enough staff now". When the search committee chairman explained the need for the youth minister, the member arose and said, "call him".

From 1981 through 2002, we had a large group of youth. This was a time when young families brought their youth to church and supported the youth programs. During these years, we were fortunate to have some good youth ministers who loved our youth and provided good programs for them. The programs included Bible studies, retreats, social activities and especially outreach to the youth community.

This was a period when the youth program included youth from the sixth grade through the twelfth. These ages extended through Sunday school, Bible study, Vacation Bible School and boys and girl mission programs. Sadly, today we are losing the seventh through the twelfth grades. Much of the problems faced by the youth today comes from worldly programs outside. Youth are attracted by what the world has to offer. But the church is also responsible for letting the world take over (Mark 19:14-19, Romans 12:2 and 1 John 4:4).

What I have said, or what I am now saying, may seem bragging, arrogant or critical but my intentions are to be helpful and thought-challenging. I hope what I have learned over sixty years of ministry will be helpful to pastors, staff and church members. I realize that much of what I am saying speaks to the problems of the total church members, but I am using these events because we are losing a total group of our youth. It's going to take pastors, staff, mothers and fathers and concerned church members to reach and save our youth from the pull of the world.

In every church that I have pastored, I have tried to have some part in every event of the church. At least every leader knew of my concern. I am well aware that the pastor cannot oversee every event. But he had better be sure that those in leadership be in charge. If he is sure, it will save him a lot of heartache.

When I came to Sweetwater, plans were being discussed about building a "gymnasium". Many were opposed because they thought it would be used for "worldly pleasures". When I suggested that it be called a "family life center", it was built and has been a blessing. This family life center has been very useful. The many events held in the family life center have helped train our youth. These events include space for classrooms for children through adults. The youth have programs such as preparing meals, special events such as athletic activities and special seminars. I will say more about athletics and other social events later.

At Sweetwater, we have had some very good youth ministers. I very much appreciate their efforts to reach and teach our youth. Our youth programs certainly were not a babysitting or play time. Too many churches expect this from youth ministers.

My ideal for a youth minister, though not perfect, is one who is called to this position, not one looking for a position. He should be one who shares the position of the pastor and church. He should support the doctrines and other programs of the church. He should be one who works closely with the pastor and shares his vision and hopes for the youth.

As a pastor I appreciated the youth minister who knew how to plan for and lead a group. My desire was for him to be a biblical teacher and one who planned retreats, seminars and other events that helped grow our youth in their spiritual walk with the Lord. Too many programs, even some by our State and Southern Baptist

Convention, are patterned after the world. Too many times the idea is to "give them what they want, not what they need".

Additional Educational Ministries

1. Discipleship Training

My how things have changed over time. When I started as a child in church, we had BYPU, it changed to BTU and is now Discipleship Training. In the beginning, from children through adults, each group met together to study their lessons. Material on particular subjects was provided. Each person had an opportunity to share in the class. I remember my precious mother getting up to give her part, and she was so nervous that her book would be shaking. But as a result, she and many others learned to stand up before a group and share.

In my opinion, Southern Baptist Churches made a tragic mistake by changing their method of training. Discipleship training is essential, but the methods used today fail to teach all members, children through adults, what we believe doctrinally, about church government and different mission programs.

When I became pastor of Sweetwater, we still used the material where members would share in the class. I enjoyed teaching Master Life. This was one of the best studies on learning scripture and doctrinal matters.

It is tragic, but true, that many Baptist members do not really know who Southern Baptists are and what we believe, what our mission programs are, what the Cooperative Program is and what Congregation Policy is all about.

I believe it would be helpful to return to the way of having training classes for all groups. This dates me and many will think of me as being old fashion, which I am, but at least we will know what we believe and why.

2. The WMU

When the Southern Baptist Convention was having the moderate and conservative dispute, some of the conservative pastors dropped the WMU Mission Program from their churches. Their reason being, they felt that convention WMU leaders were supporting the moderate group. I certainly did not believe that our WMU leadership at Sweetwater was supporting any moderate group.

Our leadership did an excellent job leading our Mission Friends, GAs and Acteens. Mission studies and Acteens of different types were provided for all age groups. I was very impressed with our leaders because they would always keep me informed about what was going on and what was about to happen.

Here again you can see that programs did not stop at the sixth grade, but programs were provided for the youth and adults. Many of our missionaries were called to service as a result of what they learned through mission programs.

3. The Brotherhood

It is clear to see that I did not mention the RAs with the WMU group. I did not, because the RAs were under the Brotherhood program where they still should be. When I was pastor, I did not know who or why the RAs were placed under the WMU but I strongly disagree with the move. Boys need the strong leadership of godly men. I am so glad that programs are still provided for children through adults.

There are rolls that the men of the Brotherhood fill. There is Bible study, mission studies, and other needs around the church. Men of the Brotherhood also make up the disaster relief teams which travel to areas in the community, state and out of the state wherever disasters have struck.

Our Brotherhood men did an excellent job with our RA boys. They provided Bible studies, mission programs, camping and other programs where the boys learned to make things with their hands.

Fishing trips were times of great excitement. The boys would catch fish and help the men clean and prepare the fish for family time together. Fathers, mothers, youth and children would enjoy fish, slaw, hushpuppies and tea together. This was an exciting time together for the church family, provided by the Brotherhood and

RAs. A special time was put on by the children and youth. I still believe times like these will still attract "youth".

It was from the men of the church that special sporting events were provided. We had softball teams for our youth, men and women. These events were used as a means of outreach and family support. We had two men's teams, a boys' team and a team for women. All of these were supported by many family members. My wife and I had to travel from game to game. One player said to me, "Preacher you will never know what it means to us to see you and Mrs. Nina at our games". At every church that I pastored, we had softball teams and I played until I got too old and then I coached or sat in the stands. If I were young and still pastored, I would play and support the team. Some churches still have teams, although the secular world has drawn many of our men and youth away. I still believe, if supported by the church, dedicated sports will still work. A church will never know unless it is tried.

Sweetwater had two men's basketball teams and a team for the youth. When the men played each other, it was like the Boston Celtics and the LA Lakers. It was a time of family fellowship and fun. Could it happen again? A church will never know if it never tries.

4. Other committees that are important to the welfare of the church are:

    a. Finance Committee

    b. Personnel

    c. Building and Grounds

    d. Trustees

    e. Benevolence

These are other committees mentioned in the constitution. The constitution authorizes how Southern Baptist Congregation Polity works. It describes how the business of the church is under the direction and control of the members as they follow the leadership of the Head, Jesus Christ (Matthew 16:18).

Chapter 43
Leaving the Parsonage
A New Home

For twelve years my family lived in the house provided by the church. It was nice, and we were happy there.

Most pastors, in years past, were satisfied to live in the homes provided by the church, while not much thought was given to the idea that the pastor might die. What would happen to the wife? A church could not afford to take care of a new pastor and the wife of the former pastor.

Before I moved to Sweetwater, I had bought land in Sumter. Long Branch, where I pastored, had discussed giving me a house allowance. I did not think much about an allowance for the next twelve years.

A friend of mine, who was in my home while conducting a revival, said, "Ben you and I are not getting any younger, have you thought about a home of your own?" Then he asked, "Would you mind if I mentioned to the personnel committee the possibility of providing you a housing allowance?" I left it up to him and he contacted the committee. The personnel committee agreed to give me the parsonage with the idea of my moving it to my land that had been so graciously provided for me. When this was presented to the deacons, they rejected the idea because they did not think it would be a good idea to move the parsonage. Their reason being that this would cause too much damage to the house and we would continually have problems.

It is amazing how God in his providence uses individuals to meet His children's needs. The church voted to provide a housing allowance based on the rental value of the parsonage.

Plans for a New Home

It seems that when hopes and dreams are the brightest, disappointment shows up. When I presented my house plans to a builder, the cost was much more than the house allowance would cover. My wife and I were heartbroken. Many times, when the hour is the darkest, God's grace and mercy take over.

For fear that I will miss some, I will not mention the names of the many who worked in the yard, on the building inside and the many things that so many did. Most of the work was free help and those who charged, did so at a reduced rate.

It is amazing how God in His sovereign way brought so many people to help. One man took over seeing the building of our home. He figured out what everything would cost and recruited all the different builders. He, his wife and my wife did all the painting and he did all the finish work. Another man brought his equipment and workers to help. Others brought in equipment to clear the space for the house. My family and I just praise the Lord for every child, youth, man and woman who help provide us with our beautiful home.

Moving In

It is very expensive to get a mover to move you from one place to another. But once again, God used church members to come to the rescue. While moving us to our new home, the many trucks traveling down Sweetwater Road made a caravan line with our furniture. This group of men saved us a lot of money and time. Many of the ladies helped Nina arrange things in the house.

Now that I am retired and have time to reflect, I am so glad that a dear friend challenged the leadership of Sweetwater Baptist Church to provide the means for us to have a home. I am so thankful that the many men and women of the church did so many helpful things to make it possible for us to have our land and home.

During Christmas, Easter and Thanksgiving, we have a house full of our sons, their wives, children, grandchildren and great-grandchildren. We have six grandchildren, three step-grandchildren and seven great-grandchildren. I baptized my six grandchildren and I would love to live long enough to baptize the others. It is my desire that all my children and their children be salt and light in this dark world. If America is to continue to be a great nation, our homes must be dedicated to the Lord. It is from the home that leaders and members of our churches, schools, work places and the world come. God bless godly fathers and mothers who raise godly children to be witnesses around the world for Jesus.

I thank God that Sweetwater has had and still has leaders and members who teach the Bible as the guide for daily living. If the satanic trend continues in America, I fear for our children and youth. Many preachers do not believe nor teach the truth of God's Word. Most schools no longer allow prayer and Bible reading in the classroom, colleges or universities, and too many in government are preaching socialism, which is one stop from communism. Many in our churches and government tolerate immorality and same-sex marriage. If these trends continue, God's judgement will come (Romans 1:18-32). God give us more preachers, teachers and government officials who will have the backbone to stand for righteousness. If we have godly homes, we will have godly people in these areas. There will always be darkness, but light outshines the darkness.

Oh, how we need revival today. When men like Dr. R. G. Lee, Dr. Criswell, Dr. Billy Graham and other great evangelists passed away, in many churches, revivals became a thing of the past. It used to be that many churches would have at least two revival meetings each year. I can remember when there were country and city-wide crusades or tent meetings. Are these types of meetings too old-fashioned, are we too busy, have we as pastors become jealous of an evangelist who might be a better speaker than us? Could this be part of the reasons that baptisms are down? I hope I am wrong about these reasons! I can remember when the evangelists would stay in the pastor's home and church members would provide meals during the week. I know that we are living in a different time and people are too busy for such today. Those days are gone, and it dates me, but I can dream of the good times of fellowship.

A lot has happened since we moved into our new home in 1992. When my mother's brother was hit and killed by a car, I moved my mother next to us. My mother never remarried after she and her husband separated. My mother worked hard to take care of me. She had to drop out of school to work on the farm, but she was determined that her son would get an education. There were times when I did not think I would make it.

Mother was excited about her new home trailer. It had all the conveniences that she had not had before. When she lived with her brother, he did not care much about those new things like air conditioners and in-door plumbing. Those kinds of modern fixtures "cost too much", according to him. Mother also enjoyed the new friends she found at Sweetwater.

Chapter 44
Preparing to Leave Sweetwater

From 1999 to 2002 was a time of soul searching. 2000 was one of the most frustrating years in my ministry. I made some decisions looking to the future of the church that pleased some and confused others. Satan used this time to cause things to be said, written and accused that certainly were not pleasing to the Lord. It did not take long for my family and me to find out who loved us. But through all the heartache, God's grace and mercy shined through for all concerned. One precious member reminded me that the "battle" was not mine but rather the Lord's. That saying meant much to Joshua and it surely did to me (2 Chronicles 20:15). Thank God for his grace and mercy in times of victory and failure.

Transition Time

It is never easy to leave a church where so many people have blessed you and given you the opportunity to minister to them. There have been good and bad times, but the good far outweighed the bad.

Why leave now? As far as I know, I am in good health. I am 66 years old and many pastors continue to pastor past that age. After a difficult time in 2000, some felt that I was not the best administrator. I never have been one to make snap judgements about decisions. In a church, that follows congregational policy, you don't make decisions the same way that a head of a company does.

My main reason for leaving Sweetwater was the fact that much was in motion for expansion and building a new building. I knew that this would be a very emotional time. For some, it would be difficult to leave the old building; for others the cost would be too great. I knew that for such a move, it would take patience, frustration, energy and the ability to keep the congregation focused on what God would accomplish in such a move. For the time it would take to complete such a building, the energy needed to lead and the ability to pay for such a project, I knew at 66 I was not the man. Too many pastors have led churches to build tremendous buildings at a great cost and then leave the church in a great debt. I knew that I loved Sweetwater too much to get them in debt and leave without completing and paying for the building.

One Year Notice

When a pastor retires, unless he is forced to retire, he usually gives the church a 30-day notice. Since I had been at Sweetwater 20 years, I gave the church a year's notice. This would give the church plenty of time to prepare a search committee for the job of searching for a pastor. When the committee was formed, they sought help and information from other church committees who recently had searched for a pastor.

Most people do not realize the hard and serious job of the committee. The member must be a dedicated, called person of God. He or she must be grounded in the doctrine of scripture and of the church. Such a person must have the needs and direction of the church in mind. This person must know what the biblical qualifications of a preacher-pastor are. Why? It is easy to doctor up a resume. A person might be the right age, have the best education, be well recommended and not be God's man for the church. Too many times church members will give the committee their views of the type of preacher they want. Their type may not be what God wants for the church, and if he is not God's man, he certainly will not be what the church needs.

As I prepared for retirement, the church prepared for my retirement. During the morning services, when I announced my retirement in a year, a precious lady, knowing the difficulties I had gone through the past year, stood and said, "Preacher I hope this will be the best year you have had." By God's grace, it was.

What A Day

How many times have you heard someone say, "I love you?" It is one thing to say it, but it is real when someone shows love.

It took love, patience and money for Sweetwater to do all they did in preparing for my retirement. The many committees did a tremendous job in preparing the events for February 16, 2002. Much of the work done by the committees was secret to me. I am sure that there were many planning meetings to decide what each group would do. It was the job of one committee to call, invite and make preparations for those invited. The social and kitchen committees worked together to prepare the fellowship hall and kitchen for the final event. The deacons made their plans for what they would do during the ceremony.

When the ceremony began, what a surprise! Members from my former church in Sumter, friends from another church in Sumter, members from North Carolina, friends who had moved away, staff members who had worked with me, my roommate from seminary and others came. The Executive Secretary of the South Carolina Baptist Convention and a dear pastor friend sent a video and letter of congratulations.

What a beautiful job the choir did. They dedicated one of the songs to Nina. That was very special because this was her special day also. She spent 21 years working in the nursery and in the choir. My precious mother and my family shared in this special time. Nina's sister, although very ill, made the trip with her husband from Sumter to be with us.

My roommate from seminary came all the way from Virginiar, and when he finished speaking, the chairman of the deacons took charge of the service. He called Nina and me to the pulpit area and after sharing some very kind words of thanks for the deacons and church for our years of service, he handed us a check. We were surprised, humbled and thankful for such a generous gift from the church. All I could say is "Thanks and I hope that over the years I have tried to show you how much I love you."

After the chairman of the search committee spoke, he told my family and me to lead the way to the family life center. What a job the kitchen and social committees had done. The decorations and different types of food were gorgeous.

A cousin of mine, who was a retired missionary, told me she had never seen anything more precious and beautiful. She was right and the memory of all the love shown will always be a special part of my memory. What a special time of fellowship we all enjoyed together. Yet, this was a bittersweet time because it had not really sunk in yet that I would not be the pastor of this great church any longer.

The secretaries put together a book filled with cards and letters from the members. The words of kindness and best wishes are such a blessing each time I read them. Even now, when I need some encouragement, I will read them and cry.

What Now

After more than 40 years of ministry, what am I going to do now? During these years, I have been on call night and day, if needed. Not to be needed, just to sit down, go to the beach or go to the mountains was not my idea of retirement. I loved to fish and hunt but not all the time. A friend of mine from the Georgia Baptist Convention asked me to send him my resume when he heard that I was retiring. I know it is a sin to worry, but that is a problem of mine. It is amazing how God works things out for us. The Sunday before I left Sweetwater, two churches had contacted me and another group from another church were in attendance on Sunday. Paul gives us great guidance for trusting the Lord (Philippians 4:6).

Chapter 45
To Silvercrest
Meeting the Church Members

My only visit to Silvercrest in South Augusta was for a funeral. The week before I left Sweetwater, the chairman of the deacons from Silvercrest called and asked if I would come and preach for them on Sunday. I agreed to preach, and I was well received by the members. The deacon chairman called on Sunday afternoon and told me that the church voted to ask me to come as their interim pastor. I agreed to meet with them and discuss with them what they expected of an interim pastor. We had a very cordial meeting. The discussion hinged on the term "full-time pastor". I let them know that I was not interested in a "full-time position" because I had just left a great full-time position. For them at this time, a "full-time position" meant sitting in the office most of the time. For the size of the church, other than special calls and visitation, full-time would mean most of the time at the church.

After our discussion together, I was asked to wait in another room while they discussed what the church could offer salary-wise and what would be expected of the pastor. The search committee at Sweetwater told me what salary they were going to offer an interim pastor and wanted to know if I thought it was a good offer. I let them know it was a very good offer and would be glad if someone would offer me such an amount. When the deacons called me back in and told me what salary they would offer, I was amazed because for their church size the salary offer was greater that what the committee at Sweetwater was offering their interim.

Getting to Work

When I met the minister of youth and music, he and I met together and discussed the needs of the church and what we could do to help meet these needs. There were homes all around the church and we decided to visit members who were not attending. During the week, a team of members, called the "Grow Team" met to send cards of invitation and encouragement to those in the community. When it came time for revival, we sent invitations to all the homes in the area. Very few people came as a result of the mailouts.

In order to encourage growth within biblical preaching, teaching Sunday school as well as all the different programs of the church were utilized. The old enemy, the devil, is always ready to destroy or hinder the work of the Lord (1 Peter 5:8). Our youth and children's programs were doing well. Trips, retreats and programs were planned, and everyone seemed to enjoy working together. Then the devil raised his old ugly head. The minister of music and youth was asked to leave because of immorality. When division happens in a church, Satan has a laughing, good time. This is especially true when the problem is caused by a pastor or staff member. No matter how good or bad the pastor or staff person is, at fault or not, members take sides. This brings confusion and pain for all concerned. In times like these, very few people ask, "what is right"; they just take sides. Satan was not finished. The couple leading the children's program got upset about something and left the church. It is amazing how people get upset over nothing.

These setbacks did not stop our youth or children. One of our members who had a fish pond invited the youth and members of the church to his pond. The young men of the youth group made a challenge to me. If I would wear my white shirt to the pond, they would wear a white shirt and tie. When I got to the pond the next day, there they stood white shirts and ties as they agreed. We had a good laugh and time together. I hope there would not be any pastor who did not have time for such an event. That same day, while I fished from the bank, a young lady came up and said, "I have trusted the Lord as my savior, and I want to be baptized and join the church". I will take time any day, at a fish pond, to meet a group of boys and hear such a request from a young lady.

Searching for a staff member is not an easy job. It is easy to doctor a resume. There are times, sad to say, when you must be very careful when accepting recommendations. Some people can be honest and yet give the wrong information about a staff person.

Silvercrest decided to look for a person who could be mentored by me to become the pastor later. Resumes were collected and one, in particular, looked good. This young man had just finished the seminary and the recommendation from the church he served sounded very positive. A time was set for him to come and meet with the deacons and me. The meeting went very well, and it appeared from our discussions with the young man that he would do well at Silvercrest. When he was asked to come for a trial meeting with the church, he agreed to come but declined to preach. According to him, he would rather give his testimony than preach. When he declined to preach, this should have been a red flag to me. Having spent three years in the seminary, he should have been able to bring a message. Since he had received a master's degree from Southern Seminary, he would have been required to have had a preaching class.

Silvercrest was patient with this young man and gave him multiple chances to succeed. But after several blunders and refusal to follow instructions, it was decided by the deacons, and church, that it was best for him to find another position.

My four and a half years at Silvercrest were very enjoyable. There were some issues, which have already been discussed, but God in His grace and mercy helped us through them. What a joy to be able to baptize more than 30 people and see some growth in the church, not just numbers, but spiritual growth.

The members of Silvercrest loved and cared for us. There were times, like our 50th wedding anniversary, that they would have a special time set aside, and they would give us gifts. When it was time for us to leave, they had a special time of fellowship and a love gift for us.

Although we have been away from Silvercrest several years, precious members still call, send cards on special events and invite us back to preach. We will always love and appreciate this great church. May God bless Silvercrest as she ministers in South Augusta, Georgia!

Chapter 46
Ministry at Red Hill
Times of Heartache

After leaving Silvercrest, a number of supply positions opened for me. During this time, I was contacted by the Red Hill Baptist Church in Edgefield about talking with the search committee. The meeting went well, but the chairman of the deacons let me know that some wanted to talk with a younger man. When that situation did not work out, I was asked to come and preach.

Situations have a way of changing our plans. Earlier I had mentioned that my mother lived close to me. One day her caregiver called and told me that mother had a terrible headache. I rushed to her home and found her in much pain. By the time I got her to the bed, she was unconscious. The ambulance arrived and it did not take long to find out that the workers were not the best. They had to call someone to come and drive the ambulance. In the emergency room, the neurosurgeon said that mother was bleeding from the brain and at her age it would be futile to operate. They put mother in a room because she was not in any pain and would not last long. Two pastor friends and two other friends were with us while others waited in another room. It was early morning, and Nina and I knew mother could not last much longer. We urged our friends to go home. They did not want to leave us but at our urging, they left. With broken hearts, Nina and I told mother to go and meet Jesus because we knew she was ready to go "home".

Mother's funeral arrangements were in Sumter where she was born. A local funeral director sent mother's body to the funeral home in Sumter. We will never forget his acts of kindness.

I reserved rooms for all the family at a hotel in Sumter for them to be at the funeral home for the viewing and the funeral on Sunday. The pastor and his wife from Sweetwater, along with members from Sweetwater, members from Silvercrest in Georgia and many friends in Sumter came to show their love for mother and our family.

As we gathered at Long Branch for the funeral, it was a sad but glorious time. I would miss my dear mother, but I knew she was with Jesus. It was difficult, but I had the main message. This is what mother would have wanted. When it came time for me to speak, I knew if Wilbur did not break down, I could make it. All the boys, Clayton and Tim loved their grandmother, but Wilbur lived by her and would take her to church. The many friends from out of town as well as local friends and relatives made things easier.

The day of mother's funeral, Red Hill was to vote for me to come as interim pastor. I was delighted that the church voted for me to come. Red Hill Baptist Church is rather unique, meaning, those who grew up in the church, and moved away, still come back and support the church. Some members pass a number of churches and still come back to Red Hill. As a result of those younger families coming back, Red Hill is fortunate to have several babies and children. Unfortunately, as the present group of young people marry, many of them will marry and move away. They will not pass other churches and still come back to Red Hill.

Red Hill is situated in an area where there is very little growth. Very seldom do you see a new home or new people moving in. Red Hill is a small church, but she is fortunate to have a group of teachers and professional members who are well-organized. This means that the different organizations are well-led.

Planning Ahead

In leading Red Hill, I used many of the methods that I had used in previous churches. Preaching was central because the Bible was the guide for the way I should live as well as the members of the church. Sunday school was the Bible teaching area for all age groups. Our mission groups were a vital part of the church outreach. The GAs, Acteens and RAs were led by very dedicated leaders. During the summer, Vacation Bible School played a very special part in teaching the Bible as well as outreach to the community. August was a special time for revival. I always tried to get the best Bible preacher and musicians possible for the revival week. These three-night meetings are not my cup of tea. When a meeting is closed on Wednesday nights, the preacher is just getting used to the people.

Working on the Building

Red Hill has a very dedicated and efficient kitchen and social committee. It did not take long to realize that the kitchen and fellowship parts of the building were too small. A building committee was formed and began to figure the best way to enlarge. The first idea brought forth was to build a new fellowship hall and kitchen. When the committee counted the cost for such a building, they decided that the cost was too great. The committee decided to ask the church to double the size of the present fellowship hall. The church voted to accept the committee's recommendation. Today the church has very comfortable fellowship as well as an enlarged kitchen. A new roof was put on the building, too.

The people at Red Hill had a desire to work. The auditorium was painted, and new stained-glass windows were installed. The parking lot was paved and when a pipe burst and flooded the auditorium, a new piano was installed, the ceiling was repaired, and part of the carpet was replaced. It was amazing to watch how all these events were paid for without the church going into debt. It just shows what can happen when God's people work together and are obedient to God in their giving.

Patient Church

How thankful I am for being the pastor of Red Hill for over 12 years. When I started, it was going to be a short time as interim, but they asked that "interim" be removed. These have been great years but the last four have been very difficult for Nina and me. It is so hurtful to see your precious loved one suffer. Things started out with a bladder problem, pneumonia and congestive heart failure, and she ended up in the hospital and rehab month after month. She was back and forth in the hospital. The doctor preformed many types of tests trying to find out what was causing all of the problems. Nina would get weak and confused. After numerous tests, the doctors decided that Nina had a problem with her liver. The doctors decided that Nina had cirrhosis of the liver. Immediately I rejected test diagnosis. I had been taught that cirrhosis was caused by drinking alcohol and I knew that this could not be true because she never drank alcohol. I was incorrect. There are other reasons why the liver can become diseased. Because of her liver problem, the ammonia level will rise and cause her to be confused. She was given a medicine to take three to four times a day to bring the ammonia level down. This medication has a terrible taste and she hates to take it.

Deep in the Valley

Problems began when Adam and Eve disobeyed God in the garden (Genesis 3:15-19). We do not understand it all but when you read the book of Job, you can see how God allowed Satan to attack Job and all that he had.

For the past four years, Nina has had a very rough time. During the first two years, she could get around by using a walker. Almost two years ago, tragedy struck again. Nina fell and crushed her hip and broke her shoulder. After surgery, she was in a rehab facility for over three months. Since coming home, she is confined to a walker and wheelchair. We have caregivers that come from 8:00 AM to 11:00 AM and from 4:00 PM to 8:00 PM. They bathe her in the morning, get her to her chair and take care of her other needs. The evening person will take care of her needs when it is time to put her to bed. From 11:00 AM to 4:00 PM Wilbur and Cathy are with us. At other times, Timothy, Tammy and their girls will help, when needed.

The Valley Gets Darker

It is a known fact that trouble finds us all. Someone said, "you are either going into trouble, in trouble or coming out of trouble." One morning Tim opened the door and said, "Clayton just shot himself." I thought it was a hunting accident. But to my horror, he had shot himself. How could this happen to someone who was so careful with guns? I knew he was usually in pain with his back and terrible headaches, but could those pains drive him to the point of taking his life? Only he and God, knew why!

In my ministry, there were numerous times when I had to tell a family that a loved one had passed away. My wife was at a missionary meeting that day. How was I going to tell her that our son had shot himself and was dead? Timothy took me to the meeting where I walked in and gave Nina the bad news. Nina and the ladies were in shock. No one knew what to say but, as well as they could, they let us know of their love and concern. When we got home, the pastor and Wilbur were there. Wilbur had Clayton's picture in his arms and would not let go of it. Timothy and Pastor Paul went to Debra, Clayton's wife. I knew he was hurting, but I was proud of Tim, the way he brought the news to all of us.

At the funeral home and service, so many showed their love and concern for Clayton's family and my family. As I spoke, our friends, church members, hunters and family, by God's grace made it possible for me to speak. As I think about the number of hunters at the funeral, I can almost hear Clayton say when we met for a rabbit hunt "Fellows, let's let daddy pray before we hunt." When the telephone would ring in the morning, I can still hear his voice as he would say, "What's up, dad, and how is mama?"

Help is Near

These past four years have been very difficult. How many times have I said, "I don't know how people make it without the Lord and a church home when trouble comes." When trouble comes to Christians, who have a loving church family, we can. Until you walk in another person's shoes, be careful of how you try to make his or her hurts go away. It is amazing how church members come to the rescue of those who are in trouble. Nina and I have been blessed by individuals bringing food, Sunday school classes bringing or sending food or gift cards. Even people from other churches have been so helpful. When bills pile in, some classes or individuals come to the rescue.

During these past years, I have had to deal with hospitals, visit rehab facilities, and see Nina go through so many tests, with so many different doctors, that I told someone that I was going to change from a doctor of ministry to a medical doctorate. When you come through our kitchen, it looks like a pharmacy.

Thank God for His grace and mercy. He gives us strength when we need it most. He understands when we are frustrated and out of patience. Satan will use sickness, pain and disappointments to defeat us if we are not careful. As God's children, we need to follow Paul's instructions (Ephesians 6:11-18).

Most Christians do not understand that God has a direct will and a permissive will. God is sovereign and can do what He wills for us. Although God can stop things from hurting us, He allows certain things to happen to us for our teaching (Romans 8:28, The Life of Job, Jonah, Paul, and 2 Corinthians 12:7-10) are examples.

During these past years in the "valley", these three areas, physical, emotional and spiritual have been a challenging time for Nina and me. Some of Nina's physical concerns have already been listed, but there are many that have not been listed. A broken shoulder, hip and poor circulation not only cause pain but cause emotional, as well as spiritual, problems. Unless you have been in a wheelchair and must have someone to bathe and dress you, it is impossible to tell the emotional strain on a person. Nina has always been very active when it comes to traveling, fishing, cooking, and canning, and I can see the emotional strain when someone else is in charge of her kitchen. She always visited the sick and those in need. Now that she cannot go, she has me call and find out about the sick. I told her that she needed to get her a secretary to do her calling. It broke my heart when she asked me, "Do you think I will ever be able to walk again?" When you are having all kinds of problems such as pain, frustration and doubt, it is easy to ask, "What have I done to cause all these problems?" Many times, in the hospital and at home, I have heard Nina cry and call on the Lord for help. During such times, the old devil will try to tell you that the Lord does not care because the prayer was not answered immediately. Nina and I both are so glad that our Lord knows "the way through the wilderness."

Physically, during the time of Nina's illness I have been battered. I lost about 40 pounds and have not been able to gain the weight back. I am not encouraged when people tell me how bad I look. One home health nurse urged me to take care of myself. She further warned, "What will Mrs. Nina do if you get sick?" My doctor told me to get out of the house and listen to the birds. I like what Paul said about exercise (1 Timothy 4:8).

Emotionally I am drained. Things happen that I do not like. When frustration sets in, patience is short, and I do not like the person I become. I know that worry is a sin, but, at times, worry takes control, and when it does Satan has a good time. At times, I am a poor Christian, husband and caregiver. I am glad that Nina knows that I love her, and she forgives me when I am at my worst.

Physical and emotional problems can weaken us spiritually. Satan has tried his best to destroy me. At times, I am frustrated with my prayer life. Sometimes it appears that my prayers do not get above the ceiling of the house. When this happens, I begin to question my faith. All these years I have been standing firm on the truthfulness and authority of the Bible. Satan has, and is, trying to get me to doubt what God says about prayer. When the old enemy tries to make me think that my prayers are unanswered, I go back to Jeremiah 33:3, Matthew 7:7-11 and Philippians 4:6-7. Satan cannot stand to hear the name of Jesus. When doubt raises its ugly head, I tell Satan to leave, in the name of Jesus. When the storms are raging, Jesus comes to the rescue (Mark 4:37-41, 1 John 4:4).

In the previous paragraph, one might think that Satan has won the victory and that I had given up on prayer and the providence of God, but such an idea is far from the truth. I will admit that the valley was, and is, mighty dark. The ship is battered, and the storm has not stilled. When I think my prayers are not answered, and I begin to doubt, the Holy Spirit will whisper, "Son do you remember back when the Father lifted you out of the valley when you thought there was no hope." I like Job because of his steadfastness (Job 13:15), Hezekiah's prayer (2 Kings 20:1-6) Paul's obedience and the promise of Jesus (Hebrews 13:5).

Nina and I understand that there are many people whose difficulties and valleys are worse than ours, but it is my prayer that what has been shared will help someone to understand that just as God has moulded clay in our lives, He can do the same for others (Psalm 40:1-3).

Retiring

There are times in our lives when we have to make decisions that are very difficult. Retiring from Red Hill was one of those times. The leadership and members had been so patient and kind. At the hospital, two of the deacons were visiting Nina and the chairman said, "preacher you take care of your wife. We will be fine." Another deacon supplied for me when I could not get there on a Sunday morning. I knew it was getting time for me to leave when I could not fulfill my responsibilities as a pastor. It was always my prayer that God would send a preacher who would be in a position where he could be at the church, when needed. God is so faithful that He sent such a preacher.

My wife and I will never forget the love and kindness shown by the members while I was pastor and when I retired. The church not only provided a love offering but gave us a great fellowship meal. Since I retired, the leaders of our mission group, I still say our, came and did their prayers as well as planting flowers they brought.

Chapter 47
Conclusion

What a God-blessed journey! As some read *Moulded Clay 1 and 2*, they may accuse the author of bragging. They would be correct. My bragging is about the sovereign Lord, who in His providence, grace and mercy, has protected, guided and loved us every step of the journey.

Have my family and I been perfect through this journey? Absolutely not! There have been mountain-top and valley experiences. In every situation, the Lord has been by us. In no way would I compare my life with that of the prophet Jeremiah, but the same God that chose him, chose me (Jeremiah 1:4-5). God chose Nina to be my wife and helper in ministry for these past 66 years (1953-2019). We had been married a short while when Nina went to the doctor, and he told her that she could not have children. Clayton (deceased), Wilbur and Timothy and our grandchildren and great-grandchildren proved that theory wrong.

What an honor it has been for me to baptize my sons and each of our grandchildren. At my age, I do not know that I will be able to baptize my great-grandchildren. It is my desire that each will come to the Lord and serve Him.

There are many things that are too hard for man, but nothing is too hard for God (Genesis 18:19). When the battle is too great for us, God takes over (2 Chronicles 20:15). This section will be somewhat repetitive, but it shows the providence of God in each step of the journey.

Clear Creek Baptist School was just what I needed spiritually and physically. I received my schooling as well as work to take care of my family. Soon after I joinrf the Hosman Baptist Church, they called me to pastor a mission they had way back in the mountains. I learned a lot from those dear people. A few months later, the Riverside Baptist Church contacted me about supplying for them. This had to be the working of the Lord because this was one of the leading churches in the community, and I was a novice. While we were there, they took good care of us, and I learned a lot. Concord called me and I was able to finish Bible school and college, and I was able to teach school for three years. This had to be the working miracles of our Lord. After seven and a half years at Concord, Siloam Baptist Church called me as pastor, and I was able to finish seminary at Southeastern. At the time, Southeastern Seminary was very liberal, but the Lord got me through. I spent almost ten years at my home church in Sumter. Although my relatives were members of Long Branch, God blessed our ministry there. The Lord opened the door for me to get my doctorate at Southern Seminary in Louisville. I have already mentioned my 21 God-blessed years at Sweetwater. Sweetwater had to be a great church to put up with me. Sweetwater is one of the greatest churches in this community. They will soon move into their new building, and I pray God's blessings on them as they reach out to their growing community. Since I retired from Sweetwater, Silvercrest Baptist Church in Augusta and Red Hill Baptist Church in Edgefield have allowed us to minister to them. They both were, and are, loved by us. We will always cherish our time at both churches.

Praise the Lord for more than 60 years as a pastor. It is amazing how many people have touched our lives over these years. As Nina and I come to the evening times of our lives, may God use each reader to be salt and light in this dark and sinful age. If you are not saved, accept Jesus while you have the opportunity. Just as the Lord is still working in me, He is working in your life. It is amazing how God can take a mound of clay and mould it into a vessel of honor!

Dr. Eleazer Benenhaley was born in Sumter, South Carolina. He is a graduate of Clear Creek Bible School (Bachelor of Science, Education), Cumberland College and Southeastern Baptist Theological Seminary (Master of Divinity), and Southern Baptist Theological Seminary (Doctor of Ministry). He pastored churches in Kentucky, North Carolina, South Carolina and Georgia.

He is married to Nina Benenhaley. They have three children. Clayton (deceased), Wilbur and Timothy. They have six grandchildren, three step-grandchildren and seven great-grandchildren.

Bibliography

Bass, Robert. *Gamecock: The Life and Campaigns of General Thomas Sumter.* New York: Holt, Rinehart and Winston of Canada, 1961.

Buechner, Frederick. *The Sacred Journey.* San Francisco: Harper and Row Publishers, 1982.

Gregorie, Anne King. *Thomas Sumter.* Columbia, SC: R. L. Bryan Company, 1931.

History of Sumter County, South Carolina. Sumter, SC: Library Board of Sumter County, 1954.

Nicholes, Cassie. "County's 'Turk' Community Unique." Sumter News, Mar. 26, 1970.

Historical Sketches of Sumter County: Its Birth and Growth. Sumter, SC: Sumter County Historical Commission, 1975.

Sumter, Thomas Sebastian. *Stateburg and Its People.* N.p.; probably published ca. 1920 in Stateburg or Sumter, SC.

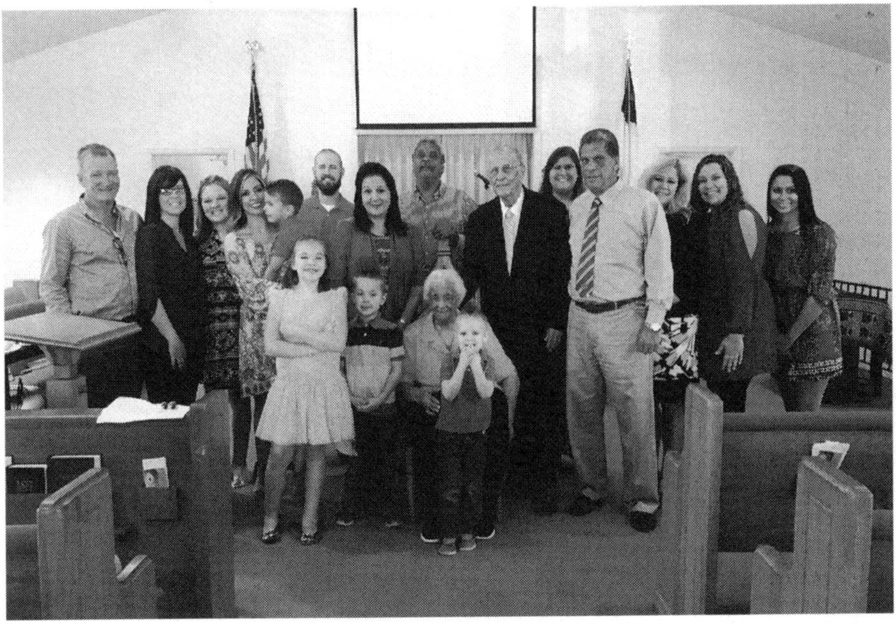

Made in the USA
Lexington, KY
30 November 2019